the food of morocco

the food of
morocco

a journey for food lovers

Text and recipes by Tess Mallos

MURDOCH BOOKS

ATLANTIC

OCEAN

SPAIN

PORTUGAL

MEDITERRANEAN SEA

Tangier

Teruan

RIF MOUNTAINS

Fez

Rabat

Casablanca

CHAOUIA REGION

Meknes

Safi

Marrakesh

ATLAS MOUNTAINS

Essaouira

DADES VALLEY

Erfoud

Agadir

SOUSS REGION

Quarzazate

Tiznit

ALGERIA

WESTERN
SAHARA

MAURITANIA

CONTENTS

FOOD JOURNEYS IN MOROCCO

the food of
MOROCCO

MOROCCO'S FOOD PEDIGREE IS ENVIABLE; WHILE THE COOKING OF THE INDIGENOUS BERBERS HAS ALWAYS BEEN A CONSTANT, AND A BASIS FOR THE CREATION OF NEW RECIPES, THE FOOD OF MOROCCO GAINED ITS UNIQUENESS THROUGH ARABIC, PERSIAN AND ANDALUSIAN INFLUENCES.

Phoenicians and Carthaginians, Romans and Byzantines all had their time in what is now Morocco. The former traded along its Mediterranean shores in ancient times, planting olive trees and vines, while the empires of Rome and Byzantium included Mauretania, as it was then known, along with the remainder of North Africa. However, it was the forces of Islam erupting from Arabia in the late seventh century that had the most enduring influence on its culture, including its cuisine. To the Arabs, the area, from present-day Tunisia to Morocco, was known as the Maghreb (furthest west), a term still in use.

While Morocco's population is eighty per cent Berber, the people are regarded as Arab-Berber. There is also a significant population of Africans from Senegal, Mauritania and Mali, a result of early trading caravans entering Morocco from across the Sahara. There are two official languages – Arabic and French, the latter from the French presence of 1912 to 1962. The French defined borders, improved infrastructure and agriculture, planted vineyards and introduced viticulture. Their food legacy is baguettes, croissants, wine, coffee and some patisserie items.

The Berbers are believed to have originated in present-day Libya, and at the time of Arab conquest, inhabited Mauretania and Numidia (in the north as far as today's Tunisia). Many of their customs continue to the present day, such as their *moussems* – festivals and pilgrimages – which

في كل ملعقة إتقان ولذة

كسكس داري ما يخطى داري

Cured olives in enamelled basins. A mosaic decorates a wall. An arched Arabian-style gateway. One of the night-time food stalls in Djemma el Fna square in Marrakesh. Not far from this city are ridges and gorges of the Middle Atlas. A woman selects her spices. Mint tea at a work site. A minaret towering behind an advertising sign for couscous – all symbols of Morocco.

A water seller in a colourfully tasselled hat. Standards fly before lines of drying cloths. A mosque stands majestically beside signs of daily life. Fish freshly grilled at the seaside. *Bissara* served for breakfast. A bowl of steamed snails. For centuries women have worn the *djellaba* – it ontrasts with modern-day activities. The orange-juice seller. Teapots. Mint tea served in a café.

last for several days. While the Berbers have their own language (with regional variations), it is not a written language. However, the culture of the Berbers today is strongly intertwined with Islam.

INFLUENCES

In 683, Arab soldiers reached Mauretania in their conquest to spread the message of the prophet, Mohammed, across North Africa. In 711, the Arabs, together with recruited Berbers, invaded the Iberian Peninsula (today's Spain and Portugal), dominating the region over the next seven centuries. As the Berbers were then known as Mauris, the invading forces collectively became known as the Moors.

The Arabs named the peninsula Al Andaluz and introduced the cultivation of the saffron crocus, various citrus fruits, figs, pomegranates, spinach, eggplants, almonds, rice and sugar cane, and these subsequently filtered down to Morocco. The full extent of Arabic culture, learning, medicine, cookery, architecture and agriculture took flower in Al Andaluz, especially under the rule of Caliph Abdu-r-Rahman III of the Caliphate of Cordoba from the tenth century. This mirrored the culture which flourished in the courts of the caliphs of Baghdad, who in turn had learned so much from the Persians they had conquered and also converted to Islam. This was the era of the *Thousand and One Arabian Nights*, a time when food was extolled in poetry, and cookery books were written.

From the eleventh century to the thirteenth century, the Berber dynasties of the Almoravides and the Almohades ruled in Al Andaluz and Morocco. The lavish court kitchens of Fes, Rabat, Meknes and Marrakesh were the conduit by which new foods were introduced and recipes refined, a process that continued with later Berber dynasties. The cuisine that evolved is unique, making the most of the ingredients Morocco produces in abundance, with flavours enhanced by new spices introduced by the Arabs. This is evident in dishes that use fruit for the sweet–sour flavours they impart, evolving into dishes that can only be Moroccan.

Traces of Ottoman cooking filtered into Morocco's north-east from Algeria, reached in the western expansion of the Ottomans. Stuffed vegetables can be attributed to this influence (the concept originating in Persia), as can the kebabs now found all over Morocco. In some cafés, especially in the north-east, Turkish coffee is available, although wherever coffee is drunk, it is usually French in style. Mint tea is the universal beverage.

9

THE FOOD OF MOROCCO

The reconquest of Spain came to an end in Granada in 1492 with the expulsion of Moors and Jews who would not convert to Catholicism. Many Jews settled in Morocco, with their recipes enriching the tapestry of Moroccan food.

With the discovery of the New World, sweet and hot peppers, tomatoes, potatoes and squash were eagerly adopted and added new dimensions to Moroccan cuisine. Dried hot, mild and sweet chillies and peppers also gave them additional spices – chilli, cayenne pepper and paprika.

FROM THE PALACES

It was in the palaces of the ruling Berber dynasties of the fourteenth century that Moroccan cooking began to take shape. The lavish court kitchens were the conduit by which new foods and recipes were eventually introduced to household kitchens. The famed *bestilla*, a pie of pigeons redolent with herbs and spices, lemony eggs and sweetened almonds, and enclosed in tissue-thin *warkha* pastry, eventually emerged – a marriage of Berber cooking and Arab influences drawn from its Persian heritage. Via the Silk Road, the Persians had learned the art of making thin pastry from the Chinese – *warkha*'s resemblance to spring-roll pastry is more than coincidental. It is made by repeatedly tapping a sticky ball of dough on an upturned *tobsil del warkha* (metal pan), lightly greased, and set over a brazier. Each rhythmic tap leaves a fine circle of dough until the entire area is one tissue-thin round. When the edge is dry, the pastry is lifted off and stacked. The *tobsil* is then upturned and used for assembling and frying the *bestilla*. *Warkha* is also used for small sweet and savoury pastries, but filo pastry and spring-roll wrappers can be substituted.

Women were always employed as cooks, and even today, in the palaces of the reigning monarch and in restaurant kitchens, women still do most of the cooking. Today the Royal Cooking School, set up by King Hussein II in his Rabat Palace complex, continues the tradition of being the training ground for future chefs, both men and women.

REGIONAL FOODS

Traditional Moroccan recipes can be found throughout most of the country. Tagines, delectable salads and couscous, from north to south, east to west, are the essence of Moroccan cooking, each cook in each region using available ingredients, determined by its history, geography and topography.

Part of an old palace. Meat at a butcher's stall. Decorative tagines. Cooking on a brazier. An Arabic gateway. The spice shop owner offering his own *ras el hanout*. Fresh peas weighed on old scales. A young girl smiles shyly. Washing hands at a fountain. With his *tangia*-filled *tangia* in hand, a young man enters the furnace room of the *hammam* (bathhouse) to have it cooked.

11

Date palms tower over the walls of Marrakesh. Fresh produce on sale. The road to Marrakesh and its famous square, Djemma el Fna; acrobats, musicians and snake charmers entertain the crowds; at night food-stalls sell typical Moroccan dishes to seated customers. An arid gorge of the Middle Atlas. Dried beans and lentils in tin bins. A young boy tends his cart of fresh mint.

مراكش

MARRAKECH
421

THE NORTH

Tetuan, Tangier and environs reflect Andalusian influences, making great use of peppers, tomatoes, olive oil, saffron and wild artichokes, and include tortilla-like omelettes and rice dishes. There are even tapas bars in these cities – vestiges of Spanish Morocco (1912 to 1956). Tetuan is also famous for its *nouga* (nougat) – another Spanish influence. In Tangier, fish is plentiful, with Mediterranean and Atlantic fish caught in its waters. In the north-west of this region, the blossoms of the *bigarade* (Seville) oranges are distilled commercially to make *zhaar* (orange flower water).

In the Rif Mountains, the Berbers are fond of *breks*, a Tunisian favourite that has been adopted by Moroccans, and make a couscous with sorghum, a grain with a buckwheat-like flavour. *Azenbu* is another popular couscous, made from green barley toasted in a pan with wild thyme, then cracked and steamed, and served with a bowl of buttermilk. *Chorba bissara*, a soup of dried broad beans, is a local breakfast staple, and a market favourite. Walnuts and chestnuts thrive, both good market crops for local souks and north coastal cities.

A famous dish of Fes is *aloes bil tamra*, using shad from the Sebou River, stuffed with almond-stuffed dates. The *bestilla* of Fes is the version prepared in most of Morocco. Tetuanese cooks look on this with disdain, claiming that Fassis cover up their mistakes with the sweet almond mixture. (In Tetuan, the filling's lemony flavour dominates.)

From the northern city of Fes to the west coast at Rabat, the Sebou Valley and the Sais Plain is rich agricultural country – the bread-basket of Morocco – producing wheat, pulses, barley, olives, sunflowers, sugar-beet, citrus fruits, grapes and vegetables, with rice grown in the irrigated Gharb region. Cattle is raised in this area but slaughtered at the yearling stage, with the beef not as full-flavoured as mature beef, and often referred to as veal.

CENTRAL MOROCCO

West of the Middle Atlas lies Marrakesh, its walls surrounded by date palms and orange groves. One of Marrakesh's famous dishes is *tangia*, a slow-cooked meat stew traditionally prepared by men. Another is *kneffa*, a festive dish of fried *warkha* pastry layered with almond custard and toasted almonds. *Tkout*, better known as *sellou*, is a mixture of browned flour, almonds, sesame and anise seeds, honey, cinnamon and butter, served in a peaked mound. Guests eat it communally with small coffee spoons.

THE FOOD OF MOROCCO

In the eastern Middle Atlas at Kelaa el M'gouna in the Dades Valley, the famous rose gardens flourish, with the fragrant fresh roses used for rosewater, the dried buds for spice stores. In Ouarzazate, where buds are distilled to make rosewater, a Rose Festival is held in mid May. Saffron is grown in the region, with its centre at Taliouine in the Anti Atlas, west of Ouarzazate. On the eastern side of the Middle Atlas, bordering Algeria, are the Erfoud Oases – Tafilalt, Rissania, Seffalat, Aoufous and Jorf – with a million date palms comprising some 30 varieties of dates.

THE WEST COAST

The Chaouia region of fertile plains on the western coast, from Rabat to Casablanca, also produces a myriad of fruits and vegetables; fields of golden wheat and sweet corn, vineyards, olive and almond groves abound. The garden continues down the southern Atlantic coast where maize, millet and barley is also grown, ending with Agadir's orange groves. Argan trees grow inland between Essaouira and Agadir and from the argan nut an oil is extracted; *amalou* is a delicious ground almond, argan oil and honey mixture, spread on bread for breakfast or snacking.

Fish and other seafoods proliferate along the coastline, benefiting from the bounty of the Atlantic Ocean. Popular dishes are *sardin mraqad* (fried sardines stuffed with chermoula), *tagine bil hout* (a fish tagine), *kseksou bil hout* (fish couscous) and *bestilla bil hout* (fish pie). Safi is famous for its *tassegal* – bluefish – with Moroccans travelling from near and far to enjoy it in its season.

THE SOUTH

The Anti-Atlas and pre-Sahara region is home to Berbers and nomadic Tuaregs. The couscous of these peoples is likely to be made from cracked barley, maize or millet, or otherwise from semolina. Meat is likely to be camel, hedgehog or wild fox, but milk and buttermilk, dates, pulses and bread made from barley, millet or wheat are their staples. *Azenbu* is another popular couscous. *Asida*, a white maize porridge, is a staple; it is taken from the communal bowl with three fingers, and dipped in melted *smen* then popped into the mouth.

FOODS FROM THE FORESTS

The forests of Morocco – in the Rif and Atlas Mountains and the Souss – have provided food for the Berbers for millennia. They continue to be a food source that adds another dimension to Moroccan food, providing acorns, pine nuts,

An apartment block with the Atlantic in view. A woman at a shuttered window. Carved fish hanging on a wall. His mint sold, a vendor wheels his cart away. Steamed snails anyone? A prized catch – crab! South-east of Essaouira, a woman cracks argan nuts. An ancient rampart in Essaouira contrasts with the modern. Camels await their cameleers. Date palms flourish in an oasis.

15

Sights in a food souk – juicy watermelons; cutting lamb cutlets; bread from a vendor; dried apricots for cooking or snacking; spices piled high in bins with rosewater and orange flower water lined up behind. The poultry seller with prepared, and yet-to-be-prepared, poultry. Making the daily bread. Rubbing cooked couscous. Vegetables await preparation for the pot.

16

mushrooms, carob, capers, wild pears, blackberries, jujube, various edible greens and wild herbs, along with the introduced mulberries.

However, the best food the forests have to offer is wild honey. It is harvested by intrepid honey gatherers who wear no protective clothing, and is sold in rural souks and at specialist honey shops; there is a particularly famous shop in the medina in Fes, where honey is sold for its sheer deliciousness and for its medicinal qualities. Carob, Atlas cedar, caper, orange blossom, saffron, thyme and lavender honey are all available. Honey is also harvested by conventional means throughout most of Morocco, with 27,000 hives producing 4,500 tonnes annually.

Prickly pear fruit (Barbary figs), regarded by Westerners as a pest, grows wild in temperate regions, and in Morocco, the delicious fruit is gathered in its season for sale in the souks, and the plants are used to fence off plots. The cactus-like plants grow in flatlands, on hillsides and in valleys.

THE MOROCCAN HOME KITCHEN

The kitchens of the *bled* (countryside) differ considerably to the kitchens in cities, which again differ from those in wealthier households. In the *bled*, they are very basic with the women of the household producing a prodigious amount of food with minimum equipment: a chopping board, knives, wooden spoons with pointed ends (the end is used for stirring, or for removing a whole chicken from a pot), a grater for preparing salads, a brass mortar and pestle for pounding spices and almonds, a sieve with a pierced metal or leather base, and a wide, shallow wooden or earthenware bowl for kneading bread, making couscous grains, or preparing couscous. Cooking over a charcoal fire is preferred for tagines; the container for the coals can be of unglazed earthenware, or a pressed steel charcoal brazier.

Pots and pans include a *couscoussier*, skillets, large soup pots and smaller saucepans of tin-lined copper, aluminium or stainless steel. Tagines of varying sizes are for family use or cooking for guests or a crowd. Spices are stored in stone jars with lids. Woven baskets are used for storing fruits and vegetables, and one with a conical lid is used for bread.

Bottled gas is widely used both in the *bled* or in cities, either as fuel for a portable gas burner, or for a cook top. The portable version is placed on the tiled floor in a corner for cooking, as is the charcoal brazier if preferred. The cook has a pad of folded carpet on which to kneel, or a low stool or thick cushion to sit on while preparing the food and cooking dishes on these floor-based cooking aids.

A city kitchen is Western in style with a Moroccan ambience, with a tiled floor, benchtops of marble and cupboards for storage; a cooking range including an oven, fuelled by bottled gas, as electricity is not considered a suitable means of cooking. These kitchens can also include a blender and a *majotte* (pressure cooker), in which tagines are often cooked then transferred to a tagine for serving.

EATING MOROCCAN FOOD

For any meal, there are rules to follow. Hands must be washed; in most households, washing hands in the bathroom is the norm, but at a formal gathering, when diners are seated at the table, a young family member or servant circulates with a jug of warm water, a basin and a linen towel. The fingers of the right hand are rinsed over the basin and dried on the proffered towel.

The table, usually round, is positioned in a corner in front of two banquettes, with chairs placed where necessary. A wedge of bread is placed before each diner generally by a daughter of the household, with more passed around during the meal. Vegetable dishes and salads are served in shallow bowls at the beginning of the meal, and are then either removed before the main meal, or left on the table to be picked at. The main meal is served in a tagine or on a large platter, placed in the centre of the table within easy reach. Morsels of food are picked from the communal dish with the thumb and first two fingers of the right hand, with food taken from the section of the dish nearest the diner. Pieces of bread are used to pick up food, soak up sauces, and wipe fingers, for fingers are never licked during the meal. Water is served during the meal, but increasingly, soda drinks are preferred.

If the dish is couscous, morsels of meat and vegetable are deftly combined with couscous and rolled into a ball, then popped into the mouth. However, spoons are also provided for those who prefer them. Hands are washed again when the meal is completed, this time more thoroughly; at formal gatherings, the water may be perfumed with rosewater, or the fragrant water is lightly sprinkled over the hands after drying, using a special flask (*rashasha*). Guests then move to the living room for mint tea and pastries.

Sweet cantaloupes in the sun. Sesame-covered bread. The hand-washing ritual. A sign advertising chicken tagines for sale. Chicken cooking over embers. Mint tea at home. Lemon verbena used to flavour mint tea. Tissue-wrapped sugar cones for the national brew. Almond-filled pastry coils and other delights at the patisserie. Young men cooling off in a rocky stream.

STREET FOOD

CHORBA BISSARA

BROAD BEAN SOUP

THE SERVING OF STREET FOOD BEGINS EARLY IN THE MORNING AND THIS DRIED BROAD (FAVA) BEAN SOUP IS A BREAKFAST STAPLE – WARMING, FILLING AND DELICIOUS. IT IS LADLED INTO BOWLS FROM A LARGE, BULBOUS EARTHENWARE JAR SET AT AN ANGLE OVER A CHARCOAL FIRE.

350g (12 oz/2 cups) dried, skinned
 and split broad (fava) beans or
 whole dried broad (fava) beans
2 garlic cloves, peeled
1 teaspoon cumin
1 teaspoon paprika
extra virgin olive oil, cumin and
 paprika to serve

SERVES 6

PUT broad beans in a large bowl, cover with 3 times their volume of cold water and leave to soak in a cool place for 12 hours, drain and rinse before cooking. (If using whole beans soak for 48 hours in a cool place, changing water 3–4 times, drain and remove skins.)

PLACE beans in a large soup pot, preferably of stainless steel. Add 1.25 litres (44 fl oz/ 5 cups) cold water, garlic and spices. Bring to the boil and simmer on low heat, covered, for 45–60 minutes, until beans are mushy; check and add a little more water if beans look dry. Do not add salt or stir the beans during cooking.

COOL slightly and then purée soup in batches in a blender, or use a stick blender and purée in the pot. Reheat soup and season to taste. Ladle into bowls and drizzle a little olive oil on each serve. Finish with a light dusting of paprika. Have extra olive oil on the table, and cumin and paprika in little bowls, to be added to individual taste. Serve with bread.

Soak dried broad beans and then skin before cooking. Ready-skinned beans are more convenient.

HARIRA

LAMB AND CHICKPEA SOUP

A POPULAR STREET FOOD SERVED WITH DATES, HARIRA IS THE BREAK-THE-FAST SOUP OF RAMADAN. THE RAMADAN HARIRA INCLUDES LENTILS AND VERMICELLI, AND IS THICKENED FOR INSTANT SATIETY AFTER A DAY-LONG FAST; DATES AND SWEET PASTRIES ARE TRADITIONAL ACCOMPANIMENTS.

500 g (1 lb 2 oz) boneless lamb
  shoulder
2 tablespoons olive oil
2 small brown onions, chopped
2 large garlic cloves, crushed
1½ teaspoons ground cumin
2 teaspoons paprika
1 bay leaf
2 tablespoons tomato paste
  (concentrated purée)
1 litre (35 fl oz/4 cups) beef stock
3 x 300 g (10½ oz) tins chickpeas
2 x 400 g (14 oz) tins chopped
  tomatoes
3 tablespoons finely chopped
  coriander (cilantro) leaves
3 tablespoons finely chopped flat-
  leaf (Italian) parsley
coriander (cilantro) leaves, extra, to
  serve

SERVES 4

TRIM the lamb of excess fat and sinew. Cut the lamb into small chunks.

HEAT the olive oil in a large heavy-based saucepan or stockpot, add the onion and garlic and cook over low heat for 5 minutes, or until the onion is soft. Add the meat, increase the heat to medium and stir until the meat changes colour.

ADD the cumin, paprika and bay leaf to the pan and cook until fragrant. Add the tomato paste and cook for about 2 minutes, stirring constantly. Add the beef stock to the pan, stir well and bring to the boil.

DRAIN the chickpeas, rinse them and add to the pan, along with the tomatoes and chopped coriander and parsley. Stir, then bring to the boil. Reduce the heat and simmer for 2 hours, or until the meat is tender. Stir occasionally. Season, to taste. Garnish with the extra coriander.

Cook the onions and garlic over low heat until the onions are soft and lightly golden.

LAMB AND FILO CIGARS

BRIOUATS ARE TRADITIONALLY MADE WITH WARKHA PASTRY AND CAN BE SHAPED INTO TRIANGLES OR CIGAR SHAPES. FOR STREET FOOD, THEY ARE ALWAYS FRIED. THE FOLLOWING RECIPE USES FILO PASTRY AS A SUBSTITUTE AND INVOLVES BAKING. IT'S EASIER TO COOK AND HEALTHIER.

1 tablespoon olive oil
1 small brown onion, finely chopped
350 g (12 oz) lean minced (ground) lamb
2 garlic cloves, crushed
2 teaspoons ground cumin
½ teaspoon ground ginger
½ teaspoon paprika
½ teaspoon ground cinnamon
pinch of saffron threads, soaked in a little warm water
1 teaspoon harissa (page 286), or to taste
2 tablespoons chopped coriander (cilantro) leaves
2 tablespoons chopped flat-leaf (Italian) parsley
1 egg
8–12 sheets filo pastry
90 g (3¼ oz) butter, melted
1 tablespoon sesame seeds

MAKES 12

HEAT the oil in a large frying pan, add the onion and cook over low heat for 5 minutes, or until the onion is soft. Increase the heat, add the lamb and garlic and cook for 5 minutes, breaking up any lumps with the back of a wooden spoon. Add the spices, harissa and the chopped coriander and parsley. Season to taste and cook for 1 minute, stirring to combine.

TRANSFER the lamb mixture to a sieve and drain to remove the fat. Put the mixture in a bowl and allow to cool slightly. Mix in the egg.

COUNT out eight sheets of filo pastry. Stack on a cutting surface with longer side in front of you. Measure and mark pastry into three equal strips and cut through the stack with a sharp knife to give strips 12.5–14 cm (5–5½ in) wide and 28–30 cm (11¼–12 in) long. Stack the strips in the folds of a dry cloth. (Use extra sheets if pastry is less than 38 cm (15 in) long.)

PLACE a strip of filo on the work surface with the narrow end towards you and brush with warm, melted butter. Top with another strip. Place 1 tablespoon of the filling 1 cm (½ in) in from the base and sides of the strip. Fold the end of the filo over the filling, fold in the sides and roll to the end of the strip. Place on a greased baking tray, seam side down. Repeat with the remaining ingredients. Brush the rolls with melted butter and sprinkle with sesame seeds.

PREHEAT the oven to 180°C (350°F/Gas 4). It is best to do this after the rolls are completed so that the kitchen remains cool during shaping. Bake the briouats for 15 minutes, or until lightly golden. Serve hot.

Brush top of folded filo strip with butter, add filling, roll once, tuck in sides and complete roll.

THE SOUK The water sellers (left) are one of the traditions of souk life, selling water to the thirsty. Wearing large-brimmed multicoloured hats festooned with tassels, their colourfully clad bodies gleam with brass-studded leather straps with clips for dangling chains, water cups, a bell and a leather water bag. Crates of live chickens (right) are ready for sale, with freshness certainly assured.

SOUKS

WHEN WALKING THROUGH THE SOUKS SITUATED IN THE MEDINAS (OLD ARAB QUARTERS) IN MOROCCO, ONE FEELS TRANSPORTED TO THE MIDDLE AGES. THE BUILDINGS, THE WARES ON SALE, THE JUMBLE OF SHOPS AND STALLS, DONKEYS CARRYING LOADS OR PULLING CARTS, THE WATER SELLERS – EACH SIGHT ACCENTUATES THE TIME WARP.

Some of the shops that line the passages of the medinas are as small as a large closet, while others are of grander proportions. Among the rows of fresh produce stalls, you might find itinerant traders sitting by their produce spread out on a cloth or displayed in baskets, with brass balance scales at the ready. The fresh meat sellers have their area, with lamb, beef, camel and goat meat on display. Spice shops and stalls, and the fresh mint sellers with stalls or laden carts add fragrance to the potpourri of aromas and – yes – smells. Smells from the live caged chickens, rabbits and pigeons permeate the souks. Shoppers move purposefully, haggling for the best price; the shouting, the braying of donkeys, the clatter of cartwheels on cobbled streets – all combine to make shopping in the souk an experience to remember.

Fresh produce abounds in market stalls; everything from young zucchini (top left) with blossoms attached to assure a special fragrance when cooked, to red onions (top centre) freshly pulled from the earth. Surrounding open-air stalls (right) there could be shops selling ornate lanterns (below left) or household items, with spice shops perfuming the air. All show the diversity of traditional Moroccan souks.

Take time out for a glass of mint tea, hot and sweet, in which to dunk a hot doughnut; or take coffee at a café with a pastry just purchased from a nearby stall (you can do that in Morocco); or enjoy a glass of freshly juiced oranges heightened with the flavour of orange flower water. Perhaps visit a shop selling milk products, better known by its French name – laiterie (*mahlaba*) – for a bowl of milk pudding (*mulhalabya*), a portion of goat's cheese or a jar of yoghurt, sold plain and very sweet, the only way Moroccans eat it. Incidentally, a delicious yoghurt called raipe is made with the dried chokes of the little wild artichokes called coque, but this type of yoghurt has its season. In any souk you can tell by the produce being sold just what time of the year it is. Not all countries are as fortunate.

QUOTBAN
LAMB KEBABS

OF ALL THE STREET-FOOD OFFERINGS, THESE WOULD HAVE TO BE THE MOST POPULAR. LITTLE CUBES OF LAMB FAT ARE PLACED BETWEEN THE MEAT TO KEEP THE LAMB MOIST AS THE KEBABS COOK OVER A CHARCOAL FIRE. THE OIL IN THE FOLLOWING MARINADE SERVES THE SAME PURPOSE.

750 g (1 lb 10 oz) boneless lamb
    from leg
1 brown onion, grated
1 teaspoon paprika
1 teaspoon ground cumin
2 tablespoons finely chopped flat-
    leaf (Italian) parsley
3 tablespoons olive oil
1 round of Moroccan bread
    (page 56) or pitta breads, to serve

HARISSA AND TOMATO SAUCE
2 tomatoes
½ brown onion, grated
1 tablespoon olive oil
1 teaspoon harissa (page 286), or
    to taste, or ¼ teaspoon cayenne
    pepper
½ teaspoon caster (superfine) sugar

SERVES 4

SOAK eight bamboo skewers in water for 2 hours, or use metal skewers.

DO NOT trim the fat from the lamb. Cut the meat into 3 cm (1¼ in) cubes and put in a bowl. Add the onion, paprika, cumin, parsley, olive oil and a generous grind of black pepper. Toss well to coat the lamb with the marinade, then cover and leave in the refrigerator to marinate for at least 2 hours.

TO MAKE the harissa and tomato sauce, halve the tomatoes crossways and squeeze out the seeds. Coarsely grate the tomatoes into a bowl down to the skin, discarding the skin. In a saucepan, cook the onion in the olive oil for 2 minutes, stir in the harissa or cayenne pepper, and add the grated tomatoes, sugar and ½ teaspoon salt. Cover and simmer for 10 minutes, then remove the lid and simmer for a further 4 minutes, or until the sauce becomes thick and pulpy. Transfer to a bowl.

THREAD the lamb cubes onto the skewers, leaving a little space between the meat cubes. Heat the barbecue grill to high and cook for 5–6 minutes, turning and brushing with the marinade. Alternatively, cook in a chargrill pan or under the grill (broiler).

IF SERVING the kebabs with Moroccan bread, cut the bread into quarters and slit each piece in half almost to the crust. Slide the meat from the skewers into the bread pocket and drizzle with a little of the tomato and harissa sauce. If using pitta bread, do not split it; just slide the lamb from the skewers onto the centre, add the sauce and fold up the sides.

For moist, tender kebabs, thread the marinated meat onto skewers and cook on a heated barbecue grill.

In Morocco, vendors mould the kefta mix deftly onto flat metal skewers. For preparing at home, make into sausage shapes, chill well and insert skewers just before cooking. Rounded skewers can 'cut' through the kefta, causing them to fall off.

QUOTBAN DEL KEFTA

KEFTA KEBABS

THESE DELICIOUS SAUSAGE-SHAPED KEBABS ARE DEFTLY TRANSFERRED INTO WEDGES OF MOROCCAN BREAD BY THE VENDORS, OFTEN DRIZZLED WITH A FIERY HARISSA AND TOMATO SAUCE (PAGE 33). THEY ARE ALSO MADE INTO SMALL, ROUND PATTIES AND CHARGRILLED.

1 small brown onion, roughly chopped
2 tablespoons chopped flat-leaf (Italian) parsley
1 tablespoon chopped coriander (cilantro) leaves
500 g (1 lb 2 oz) minced (ground) lamb or beef
1 teaspoon ground cumin
1 teaspoon paprika
¼ teaspoon cayenne pepper
¼ teaspoon freshly ground black pepper
lemon wedges, to serve

SERVES 4

PUT the onion, parsley and coriander in the bowl of a food processor and process to a purée. Add the lamb, cumin, paprika, cayenne pepper, black pepper and 1 teaspoon salt. Process to a paste, scraping down the side of the bowl occasionally.

DIVIDE the kefta mixture into 8 even portions. Moisten your hands with water and mould each portion into a sausage shape about 9 cm (3½ in) long. Insert a flat metal skewer through the centre of each kefta sausage. Place on a tray, cover with plastic wrap and refrigerate for 1 hour.

Cook on a hot barbecue grill or in a chargrill pan, turning frequently to brown evenly. The kefta are cooked until they are just well done (about 10 minutes) – they will feel firm when pressed lightly with tongs.

SERVE the kefta kebabs with lemon wedges and salad greens. If desired, provide separate small dishes of ground cumin and salt, to be added according to individual taste.

BOULFAF

LIVER KEBABS

LIVER IS HELD IN HIGH REGARD, AND IS SERVED AS FRESH AS POSSIBLE. TO KEEP IT MOIST, VENDORS INSERT PIECES OF LAMB FAT BETWEEN THE LIVER CUBES, OR WRAP EACH KEBAB WITH LAMB CAUL FAT. THE OILY MARINADE SERVES THE SAME PURPOSE, BUT DO NOT OVERCOOK.

500 g (1 lb 2 oz) lamb liver in one
   piece
1 teaspoon paprika
½ teaspoon ground cumin
¼ teaspoon cayenne pepper
2 tablespoons olive oil
1 round of Moroccan bread
   (page 56) or pitta breads, to serve
ground cumin, coarse salt and
   cayenne pepper, or 60 g (2¼ oz/
   ¼ cup) harissa (page 286), to
   serve

SERVES 4

SOAK eight bamboo skewers in water for 2 hours, or use metal skewers.

PULL off the fine membrane covering the liver. Cut the liver into 2 cm (¾ in) cubes, removing any tubes from the liver as necessary. Put the liver in a bowl and sprinkle with the paprika, cumin, cayenne pepper and 1 teaspoon salt. Add the olive oil and toss well. Set aside for 5 minutes.

THREAD five or six pieces of liver onto the skewers, leaving a little space between the pieces. Cook on a barbecue grill or in a chargrill pan, brushing with any of the oil remaining in the bowl. Cook for about 1 minute each side – the liver should remain pink in the centre, otherwise it will toughen.

IF USING Moroccan bread for the liver kebabs, cut the bread into quarters and slit each piece in half almost to the crust. For each serve, slide the liver from two skewers into the bread pocket. If using pitta bread, do not split it; just slide the liver from the skewers onto the centre and fold up the sides. Offer small separate dishes of ground cumin, coarse salt and cayenne pepper to be added to taste. If using harissa, stir 3 tablespoons hot water into the harissa and serve as a sauce.

MERGUEZ BEL FELFLA WA L'BASLA

LAMB SAUSAGES WITH CAPSICUM AND ONION

MERGUEZ, THE SPICY LAMB SAUSAGE OF THE MAGHREB, IS MUCH SMALLER THAN THOSE SOLD IN WESTERN STORES – ONLY ABOUT 8 CM (3 IN) LONG – WITH TWO SAUSAGES USUALLY SERVED ON THE ONE PIECE OF BREAD; ONE WESTERN-MADE MERGUEZ SAUSAGE IS USUALLY SUFFICIENT PER SERVE.

8 merguez sausages
1 green capsicum (pepper)
1 red capsicum (pepper)
1 large brown onion
2 tablespoons olive oil
2 rounds of Moroccan bread
　(page 56) or pitta breads,
　to serve

SERVES 4

PRICK the sausages with a fork, then cook them on a barbecue grill over low–medium heat, turning frequently, for 8–10 minutes, or until cooked through. Alternatively, cook the sausages in a chargrill pan.

MEANWHILE, cut the capsicums into quarters, remove the seeds and white membrane and cut into strips about 1 cm (½ in) wide. Halve the onion and slice thinly. Heat the olive oil in a frying pan on the barbecue, add the capsicum strips and onion and cook over medium heat, stirring often, for about 10 minutes, or until tender. If the onion begins to burn, reduce the heat to low or move the pan to a cooler section of the barbecue. Season with salt and freshly ground black pepper.

IF SERVING with Moroccan bread, cut the rounds into quarters. Place the sausages and a generous amount of the capsicum and onion mixture in the bread, or roll up in pitta bread. Alternatively, serve the sausages on plates with the vegetables, and the bread on the side.

Ensure that you frequently turn the merguez sausages to promote even cooking.

HOMUS

HOT CHICKPEAS

CHICKPEAS ARE A STAPLE IN ALL MOROCCAN KITCHENS, A MEANS OF EXTENDING THE PROTEIN CONTENT OF MEAT TAGINES AND SOUPS. AS STREET FOOD, THEY ARE SERVED IN PAPER CONES WITH A LIGHT SPRINKLING OF CUMIN AND EATEN WITH YOUR FINGERS, OR IN SMALL BOWLS WITH A SPOON.

220 g (7¾ oz/1 cup) dried chickpeas, or 2 x 420 g (15 oz) tins chickpeas
2 tablespoons olive oil
1 brown onion, finely chopped
1 small green capsicum (pepper), chopped
1 teaspoon ground cumin
2 tablespoons finely chopped coriander (cilantro) leaves

SERVES 4–6

TO COOK dried chickpeas, first soak them overnight in three times their volume of cold water. Drain and place in a saucepan with fresh water to cover well and simmer gently for 1 hour, or until tender, adding salt to taste towards the end of cooking. Drain, reserving 250 ml (9 fl oz/1 cup) of the cooking liquid.

IF USING tinned chickpeas, drain them, reserving 250 ml (9 fl oz/1 cup) of the liquid.

WARM the olive oil in a saucepan over medium heat. Add the onion and cook until lightly golden, then add the capsicum, cumin and coriander and cook for a few seconds. Add the chickpeas and their liquid, and freshly ground black pepper, to taste. Bring to a simmer, cover and simmer until heated through.

ADJUST the seasoning and serve hot in small bowls with bread.

STREET FOOD Of all of Morocco's fruits, the orange reigns supreme, evidenced by the orange-juice sellers in city squares. Vendors arrange their oranges in serried ranks for juicing to order. At night-time food stalls one might find sweet and tangy orange salads combined with carrots or olives, or mixed with dates, a sprinkling of orange flower water and cinnamon as a refreshing ending to a meal.

EATING OUT

IT IS ON THE STREETS OF MOROCCO THAT ITS CUISINE CAN BE SAMPLED AND SAVOURED. FROM THE UBIQUITOUS KEBAB TO EXOTIC STEAMED SNAILS, IT IS ALL AVAILABLE AND ON DISPLAY. AT NIGHT, IN DJEMMA EL FNA, THE FAMOUS SQUARE OF MARRAKESH, EATING OUT IS AN ADVENTURE, HEIGHTENED BY MUSICIANS, DANCERS AND ACROBATS.

However, places such as the square of Marrakesh are mainly for the benefit of tourists or out-of-town visitors. Moroccans prefer to eat at home so as not to hurt the feelings of their wives or mothers, which is not to say that they don't eat out – they do. Most city men begin the day early and breakfast on street food – it could be a bowl of broad (fava) bean soup (*bissara*), a boiled egg or two dipped in cumin and salt, or choice morsels cut from a spit-roasted lamb's head, served in bread. The doughnut (*sfenj*) makers expertly fry circles of yeast dough to crisp, golden perfection. Moroccans eat these unsugared with their breakfast soup or with glasses of sweet mint tea; otherwise, they are carried home by shoppers, strung on a loop of palm frond for a delicious morning snack.

Steamed snails (top left), cooked in a broth flavoured with caraway, liquorice root and other spices, are ladled into bowls, with little picks provided to dig out the snails; in coastal cities, fried whitebait (bottom left) is a favourite street food; lamb kebabs ready for the grill (centre), while at night-time food stalls, many of Morocco's dishes are sold, including couscous and *bestilla* (right).

The aroma of meat grilling over charcoal fires fills the air, enticing local shoppers to indulge in snacking, especially on choice foods they might not prepare at home: kebabs of lamb cubes or ground lamb (*kefta*) with a mouth-searing harissa sauce or spicy hot lamb sausage (*merguez*), slipped into bread with tomato and onion salad – such fare is only made at home for special occasions. They might also sip a bowl of lamb and chickpea soup (*harira*) with a side dish of dates, or a very sweet, honey-dipped, plaited ribbon pastry (*chebakiya*). Harira is the soup of Ramadan (the annual 30-day fast from dawn to sundown), and is only cooked at home during this most important period in the Islamic year. For tourists and travellers, street food is their introduction to Morocco's exotic cuisine.

45

ELADESS HARRA

SPICED LENTILS

MOST BROAD-BEAN SOUP SELLERS ALSO OFFER THESE SPICY LENTILS, LADLED INTO BOWLS. WHEN COOKING GREEN (ALSO CALLED BROWN) LENTILS, IT IS TEMPTING TO DRAIN THEM AFTER THE FIRST STAGE OF COOKING AS THE LIQUID IS MUDDY, BUT IN DOING SO, PRECIOUS B VITAMINS ARE LOST.

375 g (13 oz/2 cups) green lentils
2 large ripe tomatoes
3 tablespoons olive oil
1 brown onion, finely chopped
2 garlic cloves, finely chopped
1 teaspoon ground cumin
½ teaspoon ground coriander
   seeds
½ teaspoon turmeric
½ teaspoon paprika
⅛ teaspoon cayenne pepper
1 red capsicum (pepper), cleaned
   and chopped
2 teaspoons tomato paste
   (concentrated purée)
3 tablespoons chopped flat-leaf
   (Italian) parsley
3 tablespoons chopped fresh
   coriander (cilantro) leaves

SERVES 4–6

PICK over the lentils and place in a bowl. Wash with 2–3 changes of cold water, then drain in a strainer. Tip into a large saucepan and add 1 litre (35 fl oz/4 cups) water. Bring to the boil then reduce to a simmer and cook for 30 minutes, skimming the surface as required.

WHILE lentils are cooking, halve the tomatoes crossways and squeeze out seeds. Using the shredder side of a grater, grate the tomato halves down to the skin, discarding the skin. Keep aside.

WARM oil in a frying pan over medium heat, add onion and cook for 5–6 minutes or until soft. Stir in the garlic and spices and cook, stirring occasionally for 2 minutes or until fragrant. Add capsicum, grated tomatoes, tomato paste, parsley and coriander and 250 ml (9 fl oz/1 cup) water, combine well then add to the well-skimmed lentils. Season, partly cover with lid, and cook on low–medium heat for a further 25–30 minutes until lentils are tender. Serve hot in bowls.

Traditional lentils come in all hues, from green to beige to brown. Skim surfaces early in cooking.

MA'QUODA
FRIED POTATO CAKES

THESE POTATO CAKES ARE OFTEN FOUND IN THE WEEKLY SOUKS IN REMOTE REGIONS AND ARE EASY TO ASSEMBLE. POTATOES ARE USUALLY BOILED IN THEIR SKINS, BUT PEELING AND SLICING, THEN DRYING OUT THE POTATOES OVER HEAT, WORKS JUST AS WELL – MUCH KINDER ON THE FINGERS.

600 g (1 lb 5 oz) boiling potatoes
2 garlic cloves, unpeeled
1½ teaspoons ground cumin
½ teaspoon ground coriander
1 teaspoon paprika
⅛ teaspoon cayenne pepper
2 tablespoons finely chopped flat-
    leaf (Italian) parsley
2 tablespoons finely chopped
    coriander (cilantro) leaves
2 small eggs
oil for frying

MAKES 8

PEEL potatoes, cut in thick slices and place in a saucepan with water to cover. Add garlic and bring to the boil. Boil for 15–20 minutes until tender, drain and return to medium heat to dry the potatoes, shaking pan occasionally until excess moisture evaporates. Squeeze the pulp from the garlic cloves into the potatoes, then mash. Add cumin, ground coriander, paprika and cayenne pepper. Mix in lightly and leave until cool.

ADD parsley, coriander leaves and one egg to the mash and season to taste. Mix well without overworking the mash. Divide into 8 even portions. Lightly moisten hands and shape each portion into a smooth cake 1.5 cm (½ in) thick and about 8 cm (3¼ in) in diameter and place on a baking paper-lined baking tray. Beat remaining egg in a shallow dish.

IN A frying pan, add oil to a depth of 5 mm (¼ in), and place over medium–high heat. When hot, dip potato cakes one at a time into beaten egg to coat completely and fry for 2–3 minutes each side or until golden and heated through. Drain on paper towel and serve hot.

Traditionally the potatoes are cooked whole and peeled. It is quicker, and easier on the fingers if peeled and sliced before boiling. Dry by shaking pan over heat, then mash.

While Moroccan doughnut cooks have a special bent skewer to keep the hole in the doughnut, a metal skewer works just as well. To lift out put the skewer in the hole.

SFENJ

DOUGHNUTS

ALL OVER MOROCCO YOU WILL FIND DOUGHNUT MAKERS, WITH CAULDRONS OF HOT OIL, FRYING DOUGHNUTS TO ORDER. THESE ARE STRUNG ON LENGTHS OF PALM FROND AND TIED, TO BE TAKEN HOME OR TO A CAFÉ AND EATEN PLAIN WITH VERY SWEET MINT TEA. DIP IN SUGAR IF DESIRED.

2 teaspoons active dried yeast
½ teaspoon caster (superfine) sugar
375 g (13 oz/3 cups) plain
   (all-purpose) flour
vegetable oil, for deep-frying
caster (superfine) sugar, to serve
   (optional)
ground cinnamon, to serve (optional)

MAKES 20

DISSOLVE yeast in 125 ml (4 fl oz/½ cup) lukewarm water and stir in the sugar. Mix flour and ½ teaspoon salt in a mixing bowl and make a well in the centre. Pour in yeast mixture and an extra 125 ml (4 fl oz/½ cup) lukewarm water. Stir sufficient flour into the liquid to form a thin batter and leave for 15 minutes until bubbles form. Gradually stir in remaining flour, then mix with your hand to form a soft dough. If too stiff, add a little more water. Knead for 5 minutes in the bowl until smooth and elastic. Pour a little oil down the side of the bowl, turn ball of dough to coat with oil, cover with a cloth and leave for 1 hour until doubled in bulk.

PUNCH down the dough, turn out onto work surface and divide into 20 even-sized portions. Lightly oil hands and two baking trays. Roll each portion into a smooth ball and place on the trays. Using your index finger, poke a hole in the centre of each ball while on the tray, then twirl around your finger until the hole enlarges to 2 cm (¾ in) in diameter. Repeat with remaining balls of dough.

FILL a large saucepan one-third full of oil and heat to 190°C/375°F or until a cube of bread dropped in the oil browns in 10 seconds. Have a long metal skewer on hand and begin with the doughnut first shaped. Drop the doughnut into the oil, immediately put the skewer in the centre and twirl it around in a circular motion for 2–3 seconds to keep the hole open. Fry for 1½–2 minutes, turning to brown evenly. Once this process is mastered, drop 2–3 doughnuts at a time into the oil, briefly twirling the skewer in the centre of the first before adding the next. When cooked, lift out with the skewer onto a paper-towel-lined tray.

EAT while hot with mint tea or sweet coffee. While it is not traditional, toss in caster sugar, adding ground cinnamon if desired.

'ASSEER DEL LITCHINE BIL MA'ZHAAR

ORANGE JUICE WITH ORANGE FLOWER WATER

AT STREET STALLS, PERFECTLY STACKED ROWS OR PYRAMIDS OF GLOWING ORANGES ANNOUNCE THE ORANGE-JUICE SELLERS. USUALLY IT IS FRESHLY SQUEEZED, BUT ASK THAT WATER NOT BE ADDED FOR THE ULTIMATE TASTE, HIGHLIGHTED EVEN MORE WITH A DASH OF ORANGE FLOWER WATER.

6 sweet oranges
caster (superfine) sugar, to taste
1½ teaspoons orange flower water
ground cinnamon, to serve (optional)

SERVES 2

CHOOSE sweet oranges and store them in the refrigerator so they are well chilled. Using a citrus juicer, juice the oranges, then pour the juice through a sieve into a pitcher.

STIR in the caster sugar, to taste (you may not need to add any sugar if the oranges are very sweet), and add the orange flower water. Pour into two tall glasses and lightly dust the top with cinnamon, if desired. Serve immediately.

HLEEB B'LAVUKA

AVOCADO MILK DRINK

AVOCADOS ARE MAINLY USED FOR THIS DELIGHTFUL DRINK, MADE IN STREET CAFÉS AND LAITERIES USING A BLENDER. WITH BLENDERS APPEARING IN HOME KITCHENS, ESPECIALLY IN THE CITIES, THIS DELICIOUS DRINK IS OFTEN ENJOYED AT HOME. ORANGE FLOWER WATER ADDS AN EXOTIC FLAVOUR.

1 ripe avocado, about 225 g (8 oz), chilled
1½ tablespoons caster (superfine) sugar, or to taste
375 ml (13 fl oz/1½ cups) chilled milk
½ teaspoon orange flower water

SERVES 2

HALVE avocado, remove seed and, using a spoon, scoop out flesh into a blender jar. Add sugar and chilled milk. Blend until smooth and frothy. Taste and add more sugar if necessary. Add orange flower water, blend briefly and pour into two tall glasses. Serve immediately.

AVOCADO MILK DRINK

HOME COOKING

KESRA

MOROCCAN BREAD

THE FIRST TASK IN A MOROCCAN HOUSEHOLD, ESPECIALLY IN RURAL AREAS, IS MAKING THE DAILY BREAD. AS IT ONLY HAS TO RISE ONCE, IT IS QUICK TO MAKE. COUNTRY BREAD USUALLY IS MADE WITH WHOLEMEAL (WHOLE-WHEAT) FLOUR, BUT THE FOLLOWING VERSION GIVES LIGHTER LOAVES.

3 teaspoons active dried yeast
500 g (1 lb 2 oz/3⅓ cups) strong flour or plain (all-purpose) flour, preferably unbleached
200 g (7 oz/1⅓ cups) wholemeal (whole-wheat) flour
125 ml (4 fl oz/½ cup) lukewarm milk
2 tablespoons yellow cornmeal
1 tablespoon whole aniseed, toasted sesame seeds, black sesame seeds or coarse salt for topping

MAKES 3 LOAVES

DISSOLVE the yeast in 125 ml (4 fl oz/½ cup) lukewarm water. Sift the flours and 1½ teaspoons salt into a mixing bowl and make a well in the centre. Pour the yeast mixture into the well, then add 250 ml (9 fl oz/1 cup) lukewarm water and the milk. Stir sufficient flour into the liquid to form a thin batter, cover the bowl with a cloth and set aside for 15 minutes until bubbles form.

GRADUALLY stir in the remaining flour, then mix with your hands to form a soft dough, adding a little extra water if necessary. Turn out onto a lightly floured work surface and knead for 10 minutes, or until smooth and elastic and the dough springs back when an impression is made with a finger. Knead in extra plain flour if the dough remains sticky after a few minutes of kneading.

AS THE dough requires only one rising, divide into 3 even-sized pieces. Shape each piece into a ball and roll out on a lightly floured work surface to rounds 23 cm (9 in) in diameter or 26 cm (10½ in) for flatter breads.

SPRINKLE cornmeal onto baking trays. Lift the rounds onto the trays, reshaping if necessary. Brush the tops lightly with water and, if desired, sprinkle with any one of the toppings, pressing it in lightly. Cover the loaves with clean cloths and leave in a warm, draught-free place for 1 hour to rise. The bread has risen sufficiently when a depression remains in the dough after it is pressed lightly with a fingertip.

WHILE the loaves are rising, preheat the oven to 220°C (425°F/Gas 7). Just before baking, prick them with a fork. Put the breads in the hot oven and bake for 12–15 minutes, or until the bread is golden and sounds hollow when the base is tapped. Cool on a wire rack. Cut in wedges to serve. Use on the day of baking.

Roll out balls of dough, cover, leave to rise on baking trays, then prick with a fork before baking.

BEGHRIR

SEMOLINA PANCAKES

THE RESEMBLANCE TO ENGLISH CRUMPETS IS APPARENT, BUT ONCE TASTED, THERE IS NO COMPARISON. THESE LIGHT-AS-AIR PANCAKES ARE MADE WITH FLOUR AND VERY FINE SEMOLINA, RESULTING IN PANCAKES THAT BEG FOR LASHINGS OF BUTTER AND HONEY.

4 teaspoons active dried yeast
250 g (9 oz/2 cups) plain
    (all-purpose) flour
250 g (9 oz/1⅔ cups) very fine
    semolina
½ teaspoon salt
2 eggs
125 ml (4 fl oz/½ cup) lukewarm
    milk
vegetable oil, for coating
unsalted butter, to serve
warm honey, to serve

MAKES 16

DISSOLVE the yeast in 125 ml (4 fl oz/½ cup) lukewarm water and mix in 3 teaspoons of the flour. Cover with a cloth and leave in a warm place for 15 minutes until frothy.

SIFT the remaining flour, semolina and salt into a mixing bowl and make a well in the centre. Beat the eggs lightly with the lukewarm milk and pour into the flour mixture, then add the yeast mixture and 375 ml (13 fl oz/1½ cup) lukewarm water. Starting with the flour surrounding the well and working outwards, bring the flour into the liquid, beating well with a balloon whisk for 5–7 minutes until smooth. The batter should have the consistency of thick cream. Cover the bowl with a folded tea towel (dish towel) and leave in a warm place for 1 hour, or until doubled in bulk and frothy.

FILL a saucepan one-third full with water, bring to a simmer, then place a large heatproof plate over the top. Put a tea towel (dish towel), folded in quarters, on the plate.

HEAT a heavy cast-iron frying pan or crepe pan over high heat. Reduce the heat to medium and rub the pan with a wad of paper towel dipped in oil. Pour in a small ladleful (about 3 tablespoons) of batter and, using the bottom of the ladle, quickly shape into a round about 15 cm (6 in) in diameter. Work quickly and try to make the top as even as possible. Cook until the top of the pancake looks dry and is peppered with little holes from the bubbles. While it is not traditional, you can turn it over and briefly brown the bubbly side.

REMOVE the pancake to the folds of the tea towel, bubbly side up, and cover to keep warm. Overlap the pancakes rather than stack them. Repeat with the remaining batter, oiling the pan with the wad of paper towel between each pancake. Serve hot with butter and warm honey.

Use the base of the ladle to spread out the batter. These pancakes have a crumpet-like appearance when cooked.

As an alternative to the spicy meat filling, these flaky pancakes can also be filled with a sweetened, buttery ground-almond paste spiced with ground cinnamon.

REGHAIF

FILLED SAVOURY PANCAKES

THESE YEAST-DOUGH PANCAKES ARE FLAKY, LIGHT AND CRISP AS A RESULT OF CAREFUL ROLLING AND FOLDING. THE SPICED KEFTA MIXTURE IS A SUBSTITUTE FOR A PRESERVED SPICED MEAT CALLED KHLI' TRADITIONALLY USED IN MOROCCO FOR THESE DELICIOUS SNACK BREADS.

2 teaspoons active dried yeast
1 teaspoon caster (superfine) sugar
350 g (12 oz/2¾ cups) plain (all-purpose) flour
oil, for shaping and frying

SPICED KEFTA
80 g (2¾ oz) smen (page 282) or ghee
250 g (9 oz) finely minced (ground) beef
2 tablespoons grated brown onion
4 garlic cloves, finely chopped
2 teaspoons ground cumin
2 teaspoons ground coriander

MAKES 12

DISSOLVE yeast in 125 ml (4 fl oz/½ cup) lukewarm water and stir in the sugar. Sift the flour and ½ teaspoon salt into a bowl and make a well in the centre. Pour the yeast mixture into the well, then add another 125 ml (4 fl oz/½ cup) lukewarm water. Stir sufficient flour into the liquid to form a thin batter, cover the bowl with a cloth and leave for 15 minutes until bubbles form. Gradually stir in the remaining flour, then mix with your hands until a sticky dough is formed. If too stiff, add a little more water. Knead for 10 minutes in the bowl until smooth and elastic, then cover and leave in a warm place for 30 minutes.

TO MAKE the spiced kefta, heat the smen or ghee in a frying pan, add the beef and stir over high heat until browned. Reduce the heat to low, add the onion, garlic, cumin and coriander and season with salt and pepper. Cook, stirring, for 2 minutes, then add 500 ml (17 fl oz/2 cups) water. Cover and simmer for 30–45 minutes until the water evaporates and the fat separates. Tip into a food processor and process to a paste; alternatively, pound to a paste in a mortar. Set aside to cool.

USING oiled hands, punch down the dough and divide into 12 balls. Oil the work surface and a rolling pin and roll out and stretch a dough ball into an 18 cm (7 in) circle. Spread thinly with a tablespoon of kefta paste. Fold the sides in so that they overlap, then fold in the top and bottom to overlap in the centre. Roll out and shape into a 9 x 13 cm (3½ x 5 in) rectangle. Place on an oiled tray and repeat with the remaining ingredients.

IN A frying pan, add the oil to a depth of 1 cm (½ in). Place over high heat and, when almost smoking, reduce the heat to medium and add two pancakes. Cook for about 1 minute per side, or until browned and crisp and cooked through. Drain on paper towel and serve hot.

BREK BE TON

FRIED TUNA PASTRIES

TO EAT THIS TUNISIAN PASTRY (ADOPTED BY MOROCCANS), HOLD IT BY THE CORNERS, FILLING-SIDE UP, AND BITE INTO THE EGG, ALLOWING THE YOLK TO RUN INTO THE TUNA MIXTURE. WHILE SPRING-ROLL WRAPPERS ARE USED, WARKHA PASTRY IS NOW AVAILABLE IN SOME WESTERN MARKETS.

2 tablespoons finely chopped brown onion
2 teaspoons olive oil
3 anchovy fillets, finely chopped
95 g (3¼ oz) tin tuna, in brine
2 teaspoons capers, rinsed, drained and chopped
2 tablespoons finely chopped flat-leaf (Italian) parsley
olive oil, for frying
4 x 21 cm (8¼ in) square spring-roll wrappers (egg roll skins) or warkha pastry rounds
1 egg white, lightly beaten
4 small eggs

SERVES 2

IN A small frying pan, gently cook the onion in the olive oil until softened. Add the anchovies and cook, stirring, until they have melted. Tip into a bowl. Drain the tuna well and put it in the bowl, then add the capers and parsley. Mix well, breaking up the chunks of tuna. Divide the mixture in the bowl into four portions.

POUR the oil into a large frying pan to a depth of 1 cm (½ in) and place over medium heat.

PUT a spring-roll wrapper on the work surface and brush around the edge with beaten egg white. Put a quarter of the filling on one corner of the wrapper, with the edge of the filling just touching the centre of the wrapper. Make an indent in the filling with the back of a spoon and break an egg into the centre of the filling. Fold the pastry over to form a triangle and firmly press the edges together to seal.

AS SOON as you have finished the first pastry triangle, carefully lift it up using a wide spatula to help support the filling, and slide it into the hot oil. Fry for about 30 seconds on each side, spooning hot oil on top at the beginning of frying. If a firmly cooked egg is preferred, cook for 50 seconds on each side. When golden brown and crisp, remove with the spatula and drain on paper towel. Repeat with the remaining wrappers and filling. Do not be tempted to prepare all the pastry triangles before frying them, as the moist filling soaks through the wrapper.

EITHER eat the traditional way by holding the brek by the corners, or use a knife and fork.

Take care when assembling and cooking to keep egg yolk intact. Break egg into a small bowl if necessary and slide into the filling. With spring-roll wrappers, the normally semicircular pastries become triangles.

BEYSSARA

BROAD BEAN DIP

TO MAKE THIS DELICIOUS DIP, DRIED BROAD (FAVA) BEANS ARE SOAKED FOR 48 HOURS, AND THE LEATHERY SKIN IS REMOVED. FORTUNATELY MIDDLE EASTERN FOOD MARKETS NOW STOCK DRIED, SKINNED BROAD BEANS (SEE GLOSSARY).

175 g (6 oz/1¼ cups) dried broad (fava) beans or ready-skinned dried broad beans
2 garlic cloves, crushed
½ teaspoon ground cumin
1½ tablespoons lemon juice
80 ml (2½ fl oz/⅓ cup) olive oil
large pinch of paprika
2 tablespoons chopped flat-leaf (Italian) parsley
flat bread, to serve

SERVES 6

PUT the dried broad beans in a large bowl, cover with 750 ml (26 fl oz/3 cups) cold water and leave to soak in a cool place. If using dried beans with skins, soak them for 48 hours, changing the water once. If using ready-skinned dried beans, soak them for 12 hours only.

DRAIN the beans. If using beans with skins, remove the skins. To do this, slit the skin with the point of a knife and slip the bean out of its skin.

PUT the beans in a large saucepan with water to cover and bring to the boil. Cover and simmer over low heat for 1 hour, or until tender (if the water boils over, uncover the pan a little). After 1 hour, remove the lid and cook for a further 15 minutes, or until most of the liquid has evaporated, taking care that the beans do not catch on the base of the pan.

PURÉE the beans in a food processsor, then transfer to a bowl and stir in the garlic, cumin and lemon juice. Add salt, to taste. Gradually stir in enough olive oil to give a spreadable or thick dipping consistency, starting with half the oil. As the mixture cools it may become thicker, in which case you can stir through a little warm water to return the mixture to a softer consistency.

SPREAD the purée over a large dish and sprinkle with paprika and parsley. Serve with flat bread.

BOUDENJAL MAQLI
FRIED EGGPLANT JAM

ALWAYS SELECT EGGPLANTS THAT ARE HEAVY FOR THEIR SIZE. THIS INDICATES THAT THEY ARE NOT OVER-RIPE, WITH IMMATURE SEEDS FOR A BETTER FLAVOUR. SALTING DOES RID THE EGGPLANT OF BITTER JUICES, BUT CAN BE OMITTED IF YOU HAVE CHOSEN WELL.

2 x 400 g (14 oz) eggplants (aubergines), cut into 1 cm (½ in) thick slices
olive oil, for frying
2 garlic cloves, crushed
1 teaspoon paprika
1½ teaspoons ground cumin
2 tablespoons chopped coriander (cilantro) leaves
½ teaspoon caster (superfine) sugar
1 tablespoon lemon juice

SERVES 6–8

SPRINKLE the eggplant slices with salt and drain in a colander for 30 minutes. Rinse well, squeeze gently and pat dry. Heat about 5 mm (¼ in) of the oil in a large frying pan over medium heat and fry the eggplant in batches until golden brown on both sides. Drain on paper towel, then chop finely.

PUT the eggplant in a colander and leave it until most of the oil has drained off, then transfer to a bowl and add the garlic, paprika, cumin, coriander and sugar.

WIPE out the pan, add the eggplant mixture and stir constantly over medium heat for 2 minutes. Transfer to a bowl, stir in the lemon juice and season with salt and pepper. Serve at room temperature. Serve with bread as a dip, or with other salads.

Eggplants were introduced into Morocco by the Arabs via Moorish Spain, and have been part of their cuisine for hundreds of years. This fried mixture is just one of the many ways in which it is prepared.

SPICE SOUKS Of all the spices, saffron reigns supreme (bottom left), despite it being the most expensive spice of all. Some shops offer more than just spices and dried herbs; they stock gnarled roots, berries and certain desiccated wildlife, expertly ground and blended by the apothecary (centre), according to a client's ailment. Spices and dried herbs are displayed in baskets in the markets (above centre).

SPICE SHOP

ARABS WERE INVOLVED IN THE SPICE TRADE FOR CENTURIES BEFORE THEIR FORAY ACROSS NORTH AFRICA IN THE LATE SEVENTH CENTURY. VIA MOORISH SPAIN, SPICES WERE INTRODUCED INTO MOROCCO, ADDING TO THOSE ALREADY USED BY THE BERBERS. THE SPICING SKILLS OF MOROCCAN COOKS IS THE ESSENCE OF THEIR UNIQUE CUISINE.

In the spice souks, the ground spices – reds, yellows and all shades of brown – are mounded and smoothed in baskets, bins, bowls or bags. Whole spices – cassia bark and cinnamon quills, nutmeg, green cardamom pods and liquorice root, tears of mastic and gum arabic, dried chillies and fragrant dried rosebuds – contrast with the smooth mounds of the ground spices. The eight most important spices for Moroccan cooking are cinnamon, cumin, saffron (sold in small, clear plastic containers to maintain freshness), paprika, turmeric, black pepper, *felfla soudaniya* (similar to cayenne pepper) and ginger (only dried ginger is used in cooking). Then there are cloves, allspice berries, bay leaves, cumin and coriander seeds, fenugreek, aniseed and caraway seeds. As tempting as the aromas might be, Moroccan

Dried, fragrant rosebuds (bottom left) are pounded for adding fragrance to tagines, or ground by the spice merchant to add to his own *ras el hanout*. Much-loved orange flower and rosewater (bottom centre) are also available in spice shops. However, the amazing spectacle of perfect cones of ground spices (right), shaped each day with infinite care, epitomises the importance of spices in Moroccan cuisine.

cooks only purchase spices in small amounts to ensure their freshness, taking their purchases home in twisted paper packages to be stored in pottery jars.

Each spice shop has its own *ras el hanout*, which translates as 'top of the shop', or 'shopkeeper's choice'. This ground mixture may contain as many as 26 different spices and dried herbs, depending on the expertise of the shopkeeper. The mix may include black pepper, lavender, thyme, rosemary, ginger, nutmeg, cardamom, cloves, cinnamon, fenugreek and grains of paradise (melegueta pepper). Orris root, cubeb pepper, belladonna, rosebuds, hashish and other ingredients, some not available outside Morocco, might be included, depending, of course, on the shopkeeper.

This Moroccan way of preparing peeled and seeded tomatoes is worthwhile adopting. Halve crossways, squeeze out seeds, then grate – what could be easier? The flavour of this tomato jam makes any effort worthwhile.

MATISHA MAASLA

SWEET TOMATO JAM

THIS CONFIT OF TOMATOES HAS A FANTASTIC FLAVOUR. IT IS WORTH THE EFFORT USING FRESH TOMATOES, AND PREPARING THEM IN THE MOROCCAN MANNER; HOWEVER 2 X 400 G (14 OZ) TINS OF ROMA (PLUM) TOMATOES, UNDRAINED, MAY BE USED INSTEAD.

1.5 kg (3 lb 5 oz) ripe tomatoes
3 tablespoons olive oil
2 brown onions, coarsely grated
2 garlic cloves, crushed
1 teaspoon ground ginger
1 cinnamon stick
¼ teaspoon freshly ground black
   pepper
¼ teaspoon ground saffron threads
   (optional)
3 tablespoons tomato paste
   (concentrated purée)
2 tablespoons honey
1½ teaspoons ground cinnamon

MAKES 625 ML (21½ FL OZ/
2½ CUPS)

HALVE the tomatoes crossways, then squeeze out the seeds. Coarsely grate the tomatoes into a bowl down to the skin, discarding the skin. Set aside.

HEAT the olive oil in a heavy-based saucepan over low heat and add the onion. Cook for 5 minutes, then stir in the garlic, ginger, cinnamon stick and pepper and cook for about 1 minute. Add the saffron, if using, the tomato paste and tomatoes and season with ½ teaspoon salt.

SIMMER, uncovered, over medium heat for 45–50 minutes, or until most of the liquid evaporates, stirring often when the sauce starts to thicken to prevent it catching on the base of the pan. When the oil begins to separate, stir in the honey and ground cinnamon and cook over low heat for 2 minutes. Adjust the seasoning with salt if necessary.

SERVE with other salads in the traditional Moroccan way – eaten with bread at the beginning of a meal. In Morocco, this is also used as a basis for some tagines (lamb tagine with sweet tomato jam, page 112), or as a stuffing for fish. Store in a clean, sealed jar in the refrigerator for up to 1 week.

TAGINE OUMLIT BIL MATISHA
TAGINE OMELETTE WITH TOMATOES

A TYPICAL DISH MADE IN THE REMOTE MIDDLE ATLAS, USUALLY COOKED IN A TAGINE. TOMATOES ARE KEY TO THE FLAVOUR, AND TO DUPLICATE THIS, ONE WOULD HAVE TO PEEL, SEED AND CHOP A KILO OF VINE-RIPENED TOMATOES. TINNED ROMA (PLUM) TOMATOES ARE JUST AS GOOD FOR THIS RECIPE.

2 tablespoons olive oil
1 white onion, finely chopped
1 teaspoon ground coriander
1 teaspoon paprika
pinch of cayenne pepper
2 x 400 g (14 oz) tins roma (plum) tomatoes, chopped
3 tablespoons chopped flat-leaf (Italian) parsley
3 tablespoons chopped coriander (cilantro) leaves, extra to serve
8 eggs

SERVES 4

USE a 25–28 cm (10–11¼ in) non-stick frying pan with a domed lid to fit. Place over low–medium heat and add oil and onion. Cook for 6 minutes or until onion is soft. Stir in ground coriander, paprika and cayenne and cook for a further 2 minutes, Add tomatoes and their liquid, and the parsley. Increase heat to medium, season and allow to simmer, uncovered until sauce is reduced and thick – about 10 minutes.

BREAK eggs into a bowl and add 2 tablespoons water. Season and beat lightly with a fork, just enough to amalgamate whites and yolks. Pour eggs over the back of a large spoon so that the mixture evenly covers the sauce. Cover with the domed lid and cook over medium heat for 15 minutes or until set and puffed. Scatter with fresh coriander leaves and serve immediately, either cut into wedges, or spooned onto plates. Serve with bread.

TO COOK in a tagine: Make the tomato sauce in a frying pan or saucepan. Remove shelves in oven, leaving the bottom shelf in place. Preheat oven to 180°C (350°F/Gas 4). Transfer hot, cooked sauce to the tagine, cover and place in oven for 10 minutes to heat the sauce. Remove tagine from oven, immediately pour beaten eggs over the sauce, cover with its lid and return to oven for 5–8 minutes until omelette is puffed and set. Serve at the table from the tagine.

Cook the tomato sauce until reduced and thick. Pour the lightly beaten eggs over the back of a soup spoon to cover the sauce evenly.

CHORBA DJEJ BIL KSEKSOU

CHICKEN SOUP WITH COUSCOUS

USE A WHOLE CHICKEN SUITABLE FOR STEWING AND CUT IT INTO EIGHTHS, OR USE CHICKEN PIECES FOR CONVENIENCE. WHEN COOKED, THE CHICKEN MUST BE TENDER ENOUGH FOR THE MEAT TO BE EASILY REMOVED FROM THE BONES.

1.5 kg (3 lb 5 oz) chicken
2 tablespoons olive oil
2 brown onions, finely chopped
½ teaspoon ground cumin
½ teaspoon paprika
½ teaspoon harissa (page 286), or
    to taste, or ¼ teaspoon cayenne
    pepper
2 tomatoes
1 tablespoon tomato paste
    (concentrated purée)
1 teaspoon caster (superfine) sugar
1 cinnamon stick
100 g (3½ oz/½ cup) couscous
2 tablespoons finely chopped flat-
    leaf (Italian) parsley
1 tablespoon finely chopped
    coriander (cilantro) leaves
2 teaspoons chopped fresh mint
lemon wedges, to serve

SERVES 4–6

RINSE the chicken under cold running water and drain. Joint the chicken into eight pieces by first removing both legs and cutting through the joint of the drumstick and the thigh. Cut down each side of the backbone and lift it out. Turn the chicken over and cut through the breastbone. Cut each breast in half, leaving the wing attached to the top half. Remove the skin and discard it.

HEAT the olive oil in a large saucepan or stockpot, add the chicken and cook over high heat for 2–3 minutes, stirring often. Reduce the heat to medium, add the onion and cook for 5 minutes, or until the onion has softened. Stir in the cumin, paprika and harissa or cayenne pepper. Add 1 litre (35 fl oz/4 cups) water and bring to the boil.

HALVE the tomatoes crossways and squeeze out the seeds. Coarsely grate the tomatoes over a plate, down to the skin, discarding the skin. Add the grated tomato to the pan, along with the tomato paste, sugar, cinnamon stick, 1 teaspoon salt and some freshly ground black pepper. Bring to the boil, reduce the heat to low, then cover and simmer for 1 hour, or until the chicken is very tender.

REMOVE the chicken to a dish using a slotted spoon. When it is cool enough to handle, remove the bones and tear the chicken meat into strips. Return to the pan with an additional 500 ml (17 fl oz/ 2 cups) water and return to the boil. While it is boiling, gradually pour in the couscous, stirring constantly. Reduce the heat, then stir in the parsley, coriander and mint and simmer, uncovered, for 20 minutes. Adjust the seasoning and serve with lemon wedges to squeeze over, and crusty bread.

The skin is removed from the chicken before cooking as it is easier at this stage rather than when cooked.

CARROT SOUP WITH SPICES

SOUP IS OFTEN MADE FOR THE EVENING MEAL, ESPECIALLY IN RURAL AREAS, USING INGREDIENTS READILY AT HAND. IN PLACE OF THE COUSCOUS, 50 G (1¾ OZ) OF SOUP NOODLES OR CRUMBLED VERMICELLI MAY BE USED INSTEAD.

500 g (1 lb 2 oz) carrots
1 brown onion, grated
30 g (1 oz) butter
2 garlic cloves, crushed
½ teaspoon ground turmeric
½ teaspoon ground ginger
½ teaspoon cinnamon
½ teaspoon paprika
½ teaspoon cumin
pinch of cayenne pepper
1.25 litres (44 fl oz/5 cups) chicken
   stock
50 g (1¾ oz/¼ cup) couscous
2 teaspoons lemon juice
chopped flat-leaf (Italian) parsley, to
   garnish

SERVES 4

USING the shredding side of a grater, grate the carrots. Place the onion in a saucepan with the butter and cook over medium heat for 3 minutes.

ADD the garlic, turmeric, ginger, cinnamon, paprika, cumin, cayenne pepper and the grated carrot. Cook for a few seconds, then add the chicken stock.

BRING to the boil, cover and reduce to a simmer for 15 minutes. Add the couscous, stir until boiling, then cover and simmer gently for a further 20 minutes. Add the lemon juice and serve hot, topped with a little chopped flat-leaf parsley.

SPICED CARROTS

WHILE THIS IS SERVED AS AN APPETISER SALAD BEFORE A MEAL, IT ALSO MAKES AN IDEAL VEGETABLE ACCOMPANIMENT. THE SPICES ENHANCE THE FLAVOUR OF THE CARROTS AND THE LEMON JUICE COUNTERBALANCES THEIR SWEETNESS.

500 g (1 lb 2 oz) carrots, cut into
   6 x 1½ cm (2½ x ½ in) sticks
½ teaspoon paprika
½ teaspoon ground cumin
2 tablespoons finely chopped flat-
   leaf (Italian) parsley
1 tablespoon lemon juice
2 tablespoons olive oil

SERVES 4

COOK the carrots in boiling, salted water for 10 minutes, or until tender. Drain and toss lightly with the paprika, cumin, parsley, lemon juice and olive oil and season with salt.

PLACE in a serving bowl, cover and leave aside for 2 hours for the flavours to develop. Serve warm or at room temperature.

SPICED CARROTS

Gloved hands are a must when handling hot beetroot. Rub gently and the skins and stem remains slip off easily.

BEETROOT AND CUMIN SALAD

THIS WARM BEETROOT (BEET) SALAD, WITH FLAVOURS HEIGHTENED BY GROUND CUMIN, IS ONE YOU WILL MAKE AGAIN AND AGAIN. IF SERVING AS PART OF A MOROCCAN DINNER, DICE THE BEETROOT RATHER THAN CUTTING INTO WEDGES, SO THAT IT CAN BE EASILY PICKED UP WITH THE FINGERS.

6 beetroot (beets)
80 ml (2½ fl oz/⅓ cup) olive oil
1 tablespoon red wine vinegar
½ teaspoon ground cumin
1 red onion
2 tablespoons chopped flat-leaf (Italian) parsley

SERVES 4–6

CUT the stems from the beetroot bulbs, leaving 2 cm (¾ in) attached. Do not trim the roots. Wash well to remove all traces of soil, and boil in salted water for 1 hour, or until tender. Leave until cool enough to handle.

IN A deep bowl, beat the olive oil with the red wine vinegar, cumin and a good grinding of black pepper to make a dressing.

WEARING rubber gloves so the beetroot juice doesn't stain your hands, peel the warm beetroot bulbs and trim the roots. Halve them and cut into slender wedges and place in the dressing. Halve the onion, slice into slender wedges and add to the beetroot. Add the parsley and toss well. Serve this salad warm or at room temperature.

OKRA WITH TOMATO SAUCE

WHEN PREPARING FRESH OKRA, CAREFULLY TRIM THE TIP OF EACH STEM ONLY, LEAVING MOST OF THE STEM IN PLACE. IF YOU CUT INTO THE OKRA ITSELF, THE VISCOUS SUBSTANCE IT CONTAINS BECOMES MORE NOTICEABLE. ALWAYS STIR GENTLY, OR SHAKE THE PAN, DURING COOKING.

3 tablespoons olive oil
1 brown onion, chopped
2 garlic cloves, crushed
500 g (1 lb 2 oz) fresh okra, or 800 g (1 lb 12 oz) tinned okra, rinsed and drained
400 g (14 oz) tin chopped tomatoes
2 teaspoons caster (superfine) sugar
3 tablespoons lemon juice
3 large handfuls coriander (cilantro) leaves, finely chopped

SERVES 4–6

HEAT the oil in a large frying pan over medium heat, add the onion and cook for 5 minutes, or until the onion is softened. Add the garlic and cook for another minute.

IF USING fresh okra, add it to the pan and cook, stirring occasionally, for 4–5 minutes. Add the tomatoes, sugar and lemon juice and simmer, covered, for 3–4 minutes. Stir in the coriander (and the tinned okra, if used), cover and simmer for 5 minutes, then serve.

OKRA WITH TOMATO SAUCE

KHODRA BEL BARKOOK

BAKED VEGETABLES WITH PRUNES

WHILE THIS WOULD NORMALLY BE COOKED IN A TAGINE OVER A CHARCOAL FIRE, WHEN BAKED, THE VEGETABLES AND ONIONS CARAMELISE FOR EXTRA FLAVOUR, FURTHER ENHANCED WITH RAS EL HANOUT. THE PRUNES ADD A PLEASANT SWEET–SOUR FLAVOUR TO THIS DISH.

60 ml (2 fl oz/¼ cup) olive oil
2 red onions, peeled and quartered
3 garlic cloves, bruised unpeeled
2 sliced carrots
450 g (1 lb) pumpkin (winter squash)
450 g (1 lb) orange sweet potato
1½ teaspoons ras el hanout
   (page 286)
1 red chilli, seeded and sliced
375 ml (13 fl oz/1½ cups) light
   chicken or vegetable stock
200 g (7 oz/scant 1 cup) pitted
   prunes
1 tablespoon honey

SERVES 4

POUR the olive oil into a 30 x 40 x 6 cm (12 x 16 x 2½ in) ovenproof dish and add the onions, garlic and carrots. Toss well. Bake in a preheated 200°C (400°F/Gas 6) oven for 15 minutes.

PEEL and cut the pumpkin and orange sweet potato into large chunks. Add to the dish, along with the ras el hanout and red chilli. Season and toss well.

BAKE for a further 30 minutes. Stir in the light chicken or vegetable stock, prunes and honey and return to the oven for a further 30 minutes. Serve with steamed couscous or as a vegetable accompaniment.

Cut firm, peeled pumpkin into large chunks. After vegetables have partly baked, pour in the chicken stock and continue cooking.

Peeling hard pumpkin or winter squash can be hazardous if it is very firm. Use a heavy knife to cut pumpkin into large pieces. Place cut surface on a board and remove skin as shown.

MARAK GAR'A HAMRA WA BATAT HELWA

PUMPKIN AND SWEET POTATO STEW

SELECT A PUMPKIN (SQUASH) WITH FIRM ORANGE FLESH SUCH AS QUEENSLAND BLUE, KENT, BUTTERNUT PUMPKIN OR OTHER WINTER SQUASH SUCH AS HUBBARD OR TURK'S CAP, BUT AVOID THE JACK'O'LANTERN-TYPE AS ITS FLESH BECOMES MUSH WHEN COOKED.

60 g (2¼ oz) butter
1 large brown onion, finely chopped
2 garlic cloves, finely chopped
1 teaspoon ground ginger
1 teaspoon ground turmeric
1 cinnamon stick
pinch of cayenne pepper, or
    ½ teaspoon harissa (page 286),
    or to taste
500 ml (17 fl oz/2 cups) vegetable
    or chicken stock
⅛ teaspoon ground saffron threads
600 g (1 lb 5 oz) butternut pumpkin
    (squash) or other firm pumpkin
    (winter squash), peeled and
    cubed
500 g (1 lb 2 oz) orange sweet
    potato, peeled and cubed
60 g (2¼ oz/½ cup) raisins
1 tablespoon honey
coriander (cilantro) leaves, to serve

SERVES 4–6

MELT the butter in a large saucepan over low heat. Add the onion and cook gently, stirring occasionally for 5 minutes, until softened. Add the garlic, ginger, turmeric, cinnamon stick and the cayenne pepper or harissa. Stir over low heat for 1–2 minutes or until fragrant. Pour in the stock, add the saffron, then increase the heat to medium and bring to the boil.

ADD the pumpkin, sweet potato, raisins and honey and season with salt and freshly ground black pepper. Cover and simmer for a further 15 minutes, or until the vegetables are tender. Remove the cinnamon stick, transfer the vegetables to a bowl and scatter with coriander leaves.

STEWS such as this are traditionally served as a hot or warm vegetable course after the appetiser salads, but can be served as a vegetable accompaniment to the main meal. This goes well with chicken.

SHLADA MATISHA WAL HAMED MARKAD

TOMATO AND PRESERVED LEMON SALAD

WITH ITS HOT CLIMATE AND FERTILE LAND, MOROCCO PRODUCES TOMATOES THAT ARE RICHLY RED AND LUSCIOUS. THIS SALAD TEMPTS THE PALATE WITH ITS VARIED FLAVOURS. SERVE IT AS AN APPETISER IN THE MOROCCAN MANNER, OR AS AN ACCOMPANIMENT TO CHICKEN OR LAMB.

750 g (1 lb 10 oz) tomatoes
1 red onion
1 preserved lemon (page 285)
3 tablespoons olive oil
1 tablespoon lemon juice
½ teaspoon paprika
1 tablespoon finely chopped flat-leaf
  (Italian) parsley
2 tablespoons finely chopped
  coriander (cilantro) leaves

SERVES 4

PEEL the tomatoes. To do this, score a cross in the base of each one using a knife. Put the tomatoes in a bowl of boiling water for 20 seconds, then plunge them into a bowl of cold water to cool. Remove from the water and peel the skin away from the cross – it should slip off easily. Cut the tomatoes in half crossways and then squeeze out the seeds. Dice the tomatoes and put them in a bowl.

HALVE the onion lengthways, cut out the root end, slice into slender wedges and add to the bowl.

SEPARATE the preserved lemon into quarters, remove the pulp and membrane and discard them. Rinse the rind under cold running water, pat dry with paper towel and cut into strips. Add to the onion and tomato.

IN a small bowl, beat the oil, lemon juice and paprika, and add ½ teaspoon salt and a good grinding of black pepper. Pour the dressing over the salad, toss lightly, then cover and set aside for 30 minutes. Just before serving, add the parsley and coriander and toss again. If preparing this salad ahead of time, cover the bowl and place in the refrigerator, but bring to room temperature before adding the chopped herbs.

Remove pulp from preserved lemon, rinse rind, pat dry with paper towel and cut into strips.

To peel a tomato, score a cross in the base, plunge into a bowl of boiling water. After 20 seconds, transfer to cold water, then peel off skin and remove stem end as shown. To seed, cut crossways and squeeze out seeds.

CHAKCHOUKA

TOMATO, ONION AND CAPSICUM SALAD

THIS SALAD IS MADE EVERY DAY IN HOUSEHOLDS FOR THE MIDDAY MEAL. MOROCCAN PEPPERS ARE NOT AS FLESHY AS THE POPULAR CAPSICUMS (SWEET BELL PEPPERS); THEY ARE ELONGATED AND HAVE A SLIGHT PIQUANCY. IF POSSIBLE, USE VINE-RIPENED TOMATOES.

2 green capsicums (peppers)
4 tomatoes
1 red onion
1 garlic clove, finely chopped
1 tablespoon finely chopped flat-leaf
   (Italian) parsley
80 ml (2½ fl oz/⅓ cup) olive oil
1 tablespoon red wine vinegar

SERVES 4

CUT the capsicums into large flattish pieces and remove the seeds and white membranes. Place the pieces, skin side up, under a grill (broiler) and grill (broil) until the skin blackens. Turn them over and cook for 2–3 minutes on the fleshy side. Remove the cooked capsicum and place in a plastic bag, tuck the end of the bag underneath and leave to steam in the bag until cool enough to handle. Remove the blackened skin and cut the flesh into short strips. Place in a bowl.

PEEL the tomatoes. To do this, score a cross on the base of each one using a knife. Put the tomatoes in a bowl of boiling water for 20 seconds, then plunge into a bowl of cold water to cool. Remove from the water and peel the skin away from the cross – it should slip off easily. Cut the tomatoes in half crossways and squeeze out the seeds. Dice the tomatoes and add to the capsicum. Halve the onion lengthways and remove the root. Cut into slender wedges. Add to the bowl, along with the garlic and parsley.

BEAT the olive oil with the red wine vinegar and add ½ teaspoon salt and a good grinding of black pepper. Pour the dressing over the salad ingredients and toss well.

SHLADA FEKKOUS WA ZITOUN

CUCUMBER AND OLIVE SALAD

4 Lebanese (short) cucumbers
1 red onion
3 teaspoons caster (superfine)
 sugar
1 tablespoon red wine vinegar
3 tablespoons olive oil
½ teaspoon finely crumbled dried
 za'atar, or 1 teaspoon finely
 chopped lemon thyme
90 g (3¼ oz/½ cup) black olives
flat bread, to serve

SERVES 4

WASH the cucumbers and dry with paper towel.
Do not peel the cucumbers if the skins are tender.
Coarsely grate the cucumbers, mix the grated
flesh with ½ teaspoon salt and leave to drain well.

HALVE the onion and chop it finely. Add to the
cucumber, along with the sugar and toss together.

IN A small bowl, beat the red wine vinegar with the
olive oil, then add the za'atar, and freshly ground
black pepper, to taste. Whisk the ingredients
together and pour over the cucumber. Cover and
chill for 15 minutes. Scatter with olives and serve
with flat bread.

Segment an orange by
cutting between membranes.
Slice radishes on a mandolin
(vegetable slicer).

SHLADA LITCHINE WA 'L'FEGEL

ORANGE AND RADISH SALAD

3 sweet oranges
12 red radishes
1 tablespoon lemon juice
2 teaspoons caster (superfine)
 sugar
2 tablespoons olive oil
1 tablespoon orange flower water
ground cinnamon, to serve
small mint leaves, to serve

SERVES 4

CUT off the peel from the oranges using a sharp
knife, removing all traces of pith and cutting
through the outer membranes to expose the flesh.
Holding the oranges over a small bowl to catch
the juice, segment them by cutting between the
membranes. Remove the seeds from the orange
segments, then put the segments in the bowl.
Squeeze the remains of the orange into the bowl.

DRAIN the orange segments, reserving the orange
juice, and return the drained oranges to the bowl.
Set the juice aside.

WASH the radishes and trim off the roots. Slice
thinly using a mandolin (vegetable slicer). Add to
the orange segments.

PUT 2 tablespoons of the reserved orange juice in
a small bowl, add the lemon juice, sugar, olive oil
and a pinch of salt. Beat well and pour over the
salad. Sprinkle with orange flower water, toss
lightly, then cover and chill for 15 minutes. Transfer
to a serving bowl, sprinkle the top lightly with
cinnamon and scatter with the mint leaves.

ORANGE AND RADISH SALAD

THE STAFF OF LIFE Moroccans have retained many Jewish–Moroccan foods, including the *khobz chaghir*, a large bun made with white flour and smothered with sesame seeds (left). Rounds of traditional city bread, *khobz*, made with unbleached white flour, on display at a bakery (right); country bread, *kesra* or *matoula*, uses a combination of flours, and can vary in name and content from region to region.

BREAD

TO A MOROCCAN, BREAD (*KHOBZ*) IS SACRED, TO BE REVERED, SAVOURED AND NEVER WASTED. WHEN SERVED AT THE TABLE IN THE HOME, ONLY ONE OF THE FAMILY MEMBERS, USUALLY THE WOMAN OF THE HOUSE OR A DAUGHTER, DISTRIBUTES THE BREAD AS NEEDED.

One of the first tasks in most Moroccan households, especially in rural areas, is to make the dough for the daily bread. It is a simple bread, made with wholemeal (whole-wheat) flour, usually mixed with unbleached flour, and

perhaps a handful of yellow cornmeal or barley flour. Often it is flavoured or topped with caraway, anise or nigella seeds. Only water, a little salt and sugar are used in the dough, which is leavened with a sourdough starter kept from the previous day's baking, although often supplemented or substituted with active dried yeast these days. After kneading, it is shaped into flattish round loaves and placed on trays sprinkled with yellow cornmeal or semolina, covered with a cloth and left to rise only once. The loaves are stamped with each household's own mark for identification, pricked with a fork, then taken on trays to the local bakery – the marking on each loaf clearly identifying the owner. However, the baker seldom looks for the mark; he knows instinctively which tray of bread belongs to each customer.

These flattish loaves have a loose crumb that can absorb sauce, but are still crusty enough to support food as it is carried to the mouth by the fingers; the bread acting as a fork.

To make a different type of country bread, *khobz mikla*, a woman sifts white flour through a sieve into her earthenware mixing bowl. She pushes it to one side to add the dried yeast, salt and sugar and adds a little lukewarm water to dissolve the yeast. The flour is gradually worked in, adding more water to form a soft dough. It is kneaded for 10–15 minutes until smooth and elastic, then formed into four balls,

The French legacy, baguettes (left), on display at a bakery – these are almost as popular as *khobz*. Their appeal has waned little in cities, still popular with the locals and with cafés supplying baguette sandwiches to tourists. Hotels catering to tourists also use baguettes. *Khobz* (right), made in smaller rounds, are used by kebab stalls to hold kebabs and other grilled meats.

BREADS OF THE BLED

The *khobz makli* (featured below) is often made into a type of pie, simply called *makli*. Smaller balls of dough are rolled more thinly, a spicy ground meat (*kefta*) or preserved meat (*khli'*) spread on a round of dough, topped with another, edges sealed and cooked in the same way. There is also *reghaif* (page 60), which is regarded as a type of pancake but which is actually a flaky yeast bread filled with a little *khli'* or almond paste. Sweet buns called *kraiychlet*, popular in coastal towns around Casablanca, are made with an egg-and-butter-rich dough containing toasted anise and sesame seeds, and perfumed with orange blossom water, then glazed with beaten egg and sprinkled with sesame seeds before baking. Other breads of the *bled* (countryside) include an unleavened bread sheet called *therfist*, cooked on a pottery dome over embers and spread with a foamy mixture of pounded fenugreek and water. The nomadic Tauregs also bake a bread sheet on hot stones, called *tagella*.

covered and left to rise until doubled in bulk. Each round is patted out thinly. A round shallow earthenware dish (*makli*) is heated over an open fire, and a round of dough is placed in the hot dish to be cooked over the fire until browned on both sides and cooked through. The bread is often served warm for breakfast with butter and honey, or wrapped and used for the midday meal.

TAGINE OF CHICKPEAS

AN ALTERNATIVE TO TINNED CHICKPEAS IS DRIED CHICKPEAS; FOR THIS RECIPE USE 1 CUP (220 G/ 8 OZ), SOAKED OVERNIGHT IN COLD WATER, DRAINED AND COOKED WITH WATER TO COVER FOR 1–1½ HOURS. IF PREFERRED, DO NOT SKIN THE CHICKPEAS.

3 tablespoons olive oil
1 brown onion, chopped
1 garlic clove, finely chopped
1 teaspoon harissa (page 286), or to taste, or ¼ teaspoon cayenne pepper
½ teaspoon paprika
¼ teaspoon ground ginger
½ teaspoon ground turmeric
1 teaspoon ground cumin
1 teaspoon ground cinnamon
400 g (14 oz) tin chopped tomatoes
1 teaspoon caster (superfine) sugar
2 x 420 g (15 oz) tins chickpeas
3 tablespoons chopped flat-leaf (Italian) parsley
2 tablespoons chopped coriander (cilantro) leaves

SERVES 4

PUT the olive oil and onion in a large saucepan and cook over medium heat for 7–8 minutes, or until softened. Stir in the garlic, the harissa or cayenne pepper, and the spices and cook gently for 2 minutes or until fragrant. Add the tomatoes and sugar and season, to taste. Cover and simmer for 20 minutes.

MEANWHILE, drain the chickpeas and put them in a large bowl with enough cold water to cover well. Lift up handfuls of chickpeas and rub them between your hands to loosen the skins. Run more water into the bowl, stir well and let the skins float to the top, then skim them off. Repeat until all the skins have been removed.

DRAIN the chickpeas again and stir them into the tomato mixture. Cover and simmer for 20–25 minutes, adding a little more water if necessary. Stir through the parsley and coriander and season, to taste. Serve with crusty bread or with couscous.

Chickpeas are traditionally skinned for tagines so that flavours can be absorbed. Place soaked, cooked or tinned chickpeas in a bowl of water, rub handfuls together, and remove floating skins.

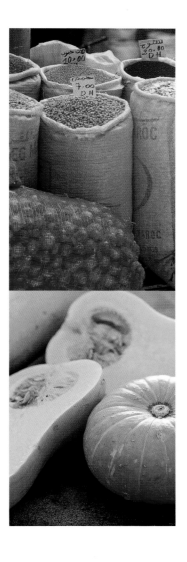

TAGINE 'ADESS BIL GAR'A HAMRA
SPICED LENTILS WITH PUMPKIN

THERE ARE FEW TRULY VEGETARIAN RECIPES IN MOROCCAN COOKING, BUT THIS IS ONE OF THEM, AND A DELICIOUS AND NUTRITIOUS ONE AT THAT. THE EARTHY FLAVOUR OF LENTILS COMBINES WITH THE SWEETNESS OF THE PUMPKIN, THE FLAVOURS MELDING WITH TRADITIONAL HERBS AND SPICES.

275 g (9¾ oz/1½ cups) green lentils
2 tomatoes
600 g (1 lb 5 oz) firm pumpkin (winter squash) or butternut pumpkin (squash)
3 tablespoons olive oil
1 brown onion, finely chopped
3 garlic cloves, finely chopped
½ teaspoon ground cumin
½ teaspoon ground turmeric
¼ teaspoon cayenne pepper, or 1 teaspoon harissa (page 286), or to taste
1 teaspoon paprika
3 teaspoons tomato paste (concentrated purée)
½ teaspoon caster (superfine) sugar
1 tablespoon finely chopped flat-leaf (Italian) parsley
2 tablespoons chopped coriander (cilantro) leaves

SERVES 4–6

PICK over the lentils and discard any damaged lentils and any stones. Put the lentils in a sieve and rinse under cold running water. Tip into a saucepan and add 1 litre (35 fl oz/4 cups) cold water. Bring to the boil, skim the surface if necessary, then cover and simmer over low heat for 20 minutes.

MEANWHILE, halve the tomatoes crossways and squeeze out the seeds. Coarsely grate the tomatoes into a bowl down to the skin, discarding the skin. Set the grated tomato aside. Peel and seed the pumpkin and cut into 3 cm (1¼ in) dice. Set aside.

HEAT the oil in a large saucepan over low heat, add the onion and cook until softened. Add the garlic, cook for a few seconds, then stir in the cumin, turmeric and cayenne pepper or harissa. Cook for 30 seconds, then add the paprika, grated tomato, tomato paste, sugar, half of the parsley and coriander, 1 teaspoon salt and freshly ground black pepper, to taste.

ADD the lentils and the prepared pumpkin, stir well, then cover and simmer for about 20 minutes, or until the pumpkin and lentils are tender. Adjust the seasoning and transfer to a serving bowl. Sprinkle with the remaining parsley and coriander leaves and serve hot or warm with crusty bread.

This leafy member of the silverbeet family has been favoured in the Mediterranean region for centuries; combining it with rice and herbs reveals Andalusian influences.

SILQ BIL ROZZ

SILVERBEET WITH RICE

CHARD (SILVERBEET) IS A POPULAR VEGETABLE THROUGHOUT THE MEDITERRANEAN REGION. IT IS A VEGETABLE THAT CHILDREN LOVE TO HATE, AND VEGETABLE GARDENERS INSIST ON PLANTING BECAUSE IT GROWS SO EASILY. THE FOLLOWING RECIPE IS AN EXCELLENT WAY TO PREPARE IT.

900 g (2 lb) silverbeet (Swiss chard)
80 ml (2½ fl oz/⅓ cup) olive oil
1 brown onion, chopped
1 teaspoon paprika
2 tablespoons chopped coriander (cilantro) leaves
2 tablespoons chopped flat-leaf (Italian) parsley
110 g (3¾ oz/½ cup) short-grain rice
1½ tablespoons lemon juice

SERVES 4

TRIM the ends of the stalks of the silverbeet. Wash well and cut the stalks from the leaves. Slice the stalks thickly and roughly shred the leaves.

HEAT the olive oil in a large saucepan and add the onion. Cook over low heat for 5 minutes, or until soft.

STIR in the silverbeet stalks and paprika and cook for 5 minutes more. Add the silverbeet leaves, coriander, parsley, rice and 125 ml (4 fl oz/½ cup) water. Increase the heat to medium and stir until the silverbeet begins to wilt.

REDUCE the heat to low, add the lemon juice and stir well. Cover and simmer for 25 minutes, or until the rice is tender, stirring occasionally. Season, to taste, and serve hot as a vegetable accompaniment.

K'DRA DJEJ

CHICKEN WITH ONIONS AND CHICKPEAS

A K'DRA IS A BERBER METHOD OF COOKING CHICKEN, CHARACTERISED BY THE LARGE AMOUNT OF HERBED SMEN (CLARIFIED BUTTER) AND ONIONS USED, AS WELL AS CHICKPEAS AND SAFFRON. THE AMOUNT OF SMEN HAS BEEN REDUCED. BUTTER CAN BE USED INSTEAD OF THE SMEN.

60 g (2¼ oz) herbed smen (page 282) or butter
3 brown onions, thinly sliced
½ teaspoon ground ginger
½ teaspoon freshly ground black pepper
1.5 kg (3 lb 5 oz) chicken, quartered
⅛ teaspoon ground saffron threads
1 cinnamon stick
2 x 420 g (15 oz) tins chickpeas
3 tablespoons finely chopped flat-leaf (Italian) parsley, plus extra, to serve
lemon wedges, to serve

SERVES 4

MELT the smen in a large frying pan. Add a third of the onion and cook over medium heat for 5 minutes, or until softened. Add the ginger, black pepper and chicken pieces and cook without browning for 2–3 minutes, turning the chicken occasionally. Add the remaining onion, 310 ml (10¾ fl oz/1¼ cups) water, the saffron, cinnamon stick and 1 teaspoon salt. Bring to a slow boil, reduce the heat to low, then cover and simmer gently for 45 minutes.

MEANWHILE, drain the chickpeas and place them in a large bowl with cold water to cover. Lift up handfuls of chickpeas and rub them between your hands to loosen the skins, dropping them back into the bowl. Run more water into the bowl, stir well and let the skins float to the top, then skim them off. Repeat until all the skins have been removed. Add the skinned chickpeas to the chicken, along with the parsley, stir gently, then cover and simmer for 15 minutes, or until the chicken is tender.

TILT the saucepan and spoon off some of the fat from the surface and put it into a frying pan. Lift out the chicken pieces, allowing the sauce to drain back into the saucepan. Heat the fat in the frying pan and brown the chicken pieces quickly over high heat. Meanwhile, boil the sauce to reduce it a little.

SERVE the chicken with the chickpeas and the sauce spooned over. Sprinkle with the extra parsley and serve with lemon wedges and crusty bread.

The browning of chicken (and lamb) after braising is a characteristic of Berber cooking. This gives an appealing golden crust on the chicken, improving presentation and flavour.

CHICKEN WITH QUINCE SAUCE

QUINCE ARE A POPULAR ADDITION TO TAGINES. FOLLOWING IS A QUICK WAY TO COMBINE FLAVOURSOME QUINCE WITH CHICKEN. WHILE THE RECIPE USES POACHED QUINCE SLICES, YOU CAN SUBSTITUTE 90 G (3¼ OZ) QUINCE PASTE; MASH IT INTO THE SAUCE AND ADD A DASH OF ROSEWATER.

1.5 kg (3 lb 5 oz) chicken, quartered
2 teaspoons ras el hanout
  (page 286)
2 tablespoons oil
1 brown onion, sliced
250 ml (9 fl oz/1 cup) chicken stock
4 slices quince in rosewater syrup
  (page 232)
1 tablespoon lemon juice
spiced carrots (page 79), to serve

SERVES 4

CUT diagonal slashes in breasts, legs and thighs of chicken portions. Rub ras el hanout into chicken, cover and leave for 20 minutes to marinate.

HEAT oil over medium heat in a large, lidded frying pan, add chicken pieces skin side down and brown lightly for 2 minutes, turn and cook for a further 2 minutes. Add onion around chicken and cook for 5 minutes until onion is soft. Add chicken stock and season if necessary with salt. Reduce heat to low, cover and simmer for 45 minutes, turning chicken occasionally.

MEANWHILE, purée quince slices with 2 tablespoons of their syrup. When chicken is tender, add the quince purée and stir into pan juices. Add lemon juice, stir well, and turn chicken in the sauce. Simmer over low heat, uncovered, until sauce is thick, about 3–4 minutes. Serve chicken with the quince sauce and spiced carrots.

By slashing the chicken almost to the bone and rubbing in the *ras el hanout*, the spices penetrate the meat in the short cooking time of this delicious dish of chicken and quince.

DJEJ MECHOUI

SPICED GRILLED CHICKEN

THE MOROCCAN SPICES AND SUGAR-DIPPED, GRILLED LEMON QUARTERS ADD AN EXOTIC TOUCH TO BARBECUED CHICKEN. PUMPKIN AND SWEET POTATO STEW (PAGE 84) GOES WELL AS AN ACCOMPANIMENT AND CAN BE COOKED ON THE BARBECUE ALONGSIDE THE CHICKEN.

2 x 750 g (1 lb 10 oz) chickens
pinch of saffron threads
1 teaspoon coarse salt
2 garlic cloves, chopped
1½ teaspoons paprika
¼ teaspoon cayenne pepper
2 teaspoons ground cumin
½ teaspoon freshly ground black
  pepper
1 tablespoon lemon juice
1 tablespoon olive oil
2 lemons
2 tablespoons icing (confectioners')
  sugar
watercress, picked over, to serve

SERVES 4

TO PREPARE the chickens, cut them on each side of the backbone using poultry shears or kitchen scissors. Rinse the chickens and dry with paper towels. Open out on a board, skin side up, and press down with the heel of your hand on the top of each breast to break the breastbone and to flatten it. Cut deep slashes diagonally in each breast and on the legs. Using two long metal skewers for each chicken, push the skewers from the tip of each breast through to the underside of the legs, which should be spread outwards so that the thickness of the chicken is as even as possible.

PUT the saffron in a mortar with the salt and pound with a pestle to pulverise the threads. Add the garlic and pound to a paste. Work in the paprika, cayenne pepper, cumin, black pepper, lemon juice and olive oil. Rub the spice mix into the chickens, rubbing it into the slashes. Cover and marinate in the refrigerator for at least 2 hours, or overnight. Bring the chickens to room temperature 1 hour before cooking.

PREPARE a charcoal fire or preheat the barbecue and place the chickens on the grill, skin side up. Cook over medium heat for 20 minutes, continually turning the chicken as it cooks and brushing with any remaining marinade. The chicken is cooked if the juices run clear when the thigh is pierced. Cooking time can be shortened on a barbecue if a roasting tin is inverted over the chickens to act as a mini oven – reduce the heat to low to prevent burning. Transfer the chickens to a platter, remove the skewers, cover with a foil tent and leave to rest for 5 minutes before cutting in half to serve.

QUARTER the lemons and dip the cut surfaces in the sifted icing sugar. Place on the barbecue hotplate. Cook briefly on the cut surfaces until golden and caramelised. Serve the chickens with the lemon quarters and watercress.

The opened-out (spatchcocked) chicken cooks more quickly on the barbecue grill, with skewers helping to keep it flat. Pound the garlic–spice mix in a mortar with a pestle as they do in Morocco.

TAGINE KEFTA 'MCHERMEL
MEATBALLS WITH HERBS AND LEMON

THE MEATBALLS IN THIS DISH, TAGINE KEFTA 'MCHERMEL, DO NOT NEED TO BE BROWNED. SPICES, COMBINED WITH FRESH FLAT-LEAF PARSLEY AND CORIANDER, AND THE HEAT OF FRESH CHILLI, ARE USED WITH LEMON TO MAKE A DELICIOUS SAUCE IN WHICH TO COOK THEM.

½ brown onion, roughly chopped
2 tablespoons roughly chopped flat-
  leaf (Italian) parsley
2 slices white bread, crusts
  removed
1 egg
500 g (1 lb 2 oz) minced (ground)
  lamb or beef
½ teaspoon ground cumin
½ teaspoon paprika
½ teaspoon freshly ground black
  pepper

HERB AND LEMON SAUCE
1 tablespoon butter or oil
½ brown onion, finely chopped
½ teaspoon paprika
½ teaspoon ground turmeric
¼ teaspoon ground cumin
1 red chilli, seeded and sliced, or
  ¼ teaspoon cayenne pepper
375 ml (13 fl oz/1½ cups) chicken
  stock or water
2 tablespoons chopped coriander
  (cilantro) leaves
2 tablespoons chopped flat-leaf
  (Italian) parsley
2 tablespoons lemon juice
½ preserved lemon (page 285)
  (optional)

SERVES 4

A food processor makes short work of the meatball mix. The combination of both lemon juice and preserved lemon adds to the appeal of this dish.

PUT the onion and parsley in the food processor bowl and process until finely chopped. Tear the bread into pieces, add to the bowl with the egg and process briefly. Add the meat, cumin, paprika, black pepper and 1 teaspoon salt and process to a thick paste, scraping down the side of the bowl occasionally. Alternatively, grate the onion, chop the parsley, crumb the bread and add to the mince in a bowl with the egg, spices and seasoning. Knead until paste-like in consistency.

WITH moistened hands, shape the mixture into walnut-sized balls and place them on a tray. Cover and refrigerate until required.

TO MAKE the herb and lemon sauce, heat the butter or oil in a saucepan and add the onion. Cook over low heat for 8 minutes until softened. Add the paprika, turmeric, cumin and chilli or cayenne pepper and cook, stirring, for 1 minute. Add the stock and coriander and bring to the boil.

ADD the meatballs, shaking the pan so that they settle into the sauce. Cover and simmer for 45 minutes. Add most of the parsley and the lemon juice and season if necessary. Return to the simmer for 2 minutes. If using preserved lemon, rinse well under running water, remove and discard the pulp and membrane and cut the rind into strips. Add to the meatballs. Transfer to a tagine or bowl, scatter with the remaining parsley and serve with crusty bread.

'L'KHODRA MAAMERA BEL KEFTA

VEGETABLES WITH LAMB STUFFING

HERE IS ONE VERSION OF MOROCCAN STUFFED VEGETABLES. MOROCCAN COOKS TAKE THE TIME TO HOLLOW OUT THE WHOLE ZUCCHINI (COURGETTES) BEFORE FILLING THEM, BUT IT IS ACCEPTABLE TO HALVE THEM, SCOOP OUT THE CENTRES, FILL THEM WITH THE STUFFING AND RE-ASSEMBLE.

4 zucchini (courgettes)
2 small capsicums (peppers)
6 tomatoes

LAMB STUFFING
2 tablespoons olive oil
1 brown onion, finely chopped
2 garlic cloves, finely chopped
½ teaspoon ground ginger
½ teaspoon ground cinnamon
¼ teaspoon freshly ground black
    pepper
500 g (1 lb 2 oz) minced (ground)
    lamb or beef
2 tablespoons chopped flat-leaf
    (Italian) parsley
1 tablespoon chopped coriander
    (cilantro) leaves
2 teaspoons chopped mint
55 g (2 oz/¼ cup) short-grain rice

TOMATO SAUCE
1 tablespoon olive oil
1 brown onion, coarsely grated
1 garlic clove, finely chopped
½ teaspoon paprika
¼ teaspoon ground cumin
1 large tomato, peeled, seeded and
    chopped
2 tablespoons tomato paste
    (concentrated purée)
1 teaspoon caster (superfine) sugar
1 tablespoon lemon juice

SERVES 4

HALVE the zucchini lengthways. Scoop out the centres, leaving a 1 cm (½ in) border. Halve the capsicums lengthways; remove the seeds and membranes. Slice the tops from four tomatoes (reserve the tops), scoop out the centres and rub the pulp through a sieve into a bowl. Remove the skin from the remaining tomatoes (page 88), slice them thinly and set aside.

TO MAKE the stuffing, put the oil and onion in a saucepan over medium heat and cook for 5 minutes. Stir in the garlic, ginger, cinnamon, pepper and add meat, stirring well to break up lumps. Add 250 ml (9 fl oz/1 cup) water, parsley, coriander, mint and 1 teaspoon salt. Bring to the boil, then cover and simmer over low heat for 20 minutes. Stir in the rice, cover, and cook for 10 minutes, or until most of the liquid is absorbed.

TO MAKE the sauce, add all the sauce ingredients and 125 ml (4 fl oz/½ cup) water to the tomato pulp. Season. Preheat the oven to 180°C (350°F/Gas 4).

LOOSELY fill the vegetables with the stuffing: fill four zucchini halves and top with an unfilled half, securing with wooden cocktail picks; fill the capsicums and arrange tomato slices over the top; fill the tomatoes and replace the tops. Arrange in an ovenproof dish. Pour in the sauce, cover with foil and bake for 50 minutes, then remove the foil, baste with sauce and cook for 10 minutes, or until tender. Remove the picks from the zucchini and serve.

Scoop out zucchini, fill and re-assemble. For capsicums, fill and top with sliced tomato.

LAMB TAGINE WITH SWEET TOMATO JAM

TOMATO JAM IS SERVED AS AN APPETISER, LIKE A DIP, BUT THE SAME INGREDIENTS COMBINE WITH LAMB TO GIVE A BEAUTIFULLY FLAVOURED TAGINE, REDOLENT OF CINNAMON AND HONEY. IT IS PREFERABLE TO USE FRESH TOMATOES RATHER THAN TINNED.

1.5 kg (3 lb 5 oz) ripe tomatoes
1 kg (2 lb 4 oz) lamb shoulder or leg
    steaks
2 tablespoons olive oil
2 brown onions, coarsely grated
2 garlic cloves, finely chopped
1 teaspoon ground ginger
¼ teaspoon freshly ground black
    pepper
1 cinnamon stick
⅛ teaspoon ground saffron threads
3 tablespoons tomato paste
    (concentrated purée)
2 tablespoons honey
1½ teaspoons ground cinnamon
30 g (1 oz) butter
40 g (1½ oz/¼ cup) blanched
    almonds

SERVES 4–6

HALVE the tomatoes crossways and squeeze out the seeds. Coarsely grate the tomatoes into a bowl down to the skin, discarding the skin. Set aside.

TRIM the lamb steaks and cut into 3 cm (1¼ in) pieces. Heat half the olive oil in a heavy-based saucepan over high heat and brown the lamb on each side, in batches. Set aside on a plate.

REDUCE the heat to low, add the remaining olive oil and the onion and cook gently, stirring occasionally, for 10 minutes, or until the onion has softened. Stir in the garlic, ginger, black pepper and cinnamon stick and cook for 1 minute. Add the saffron and the tomato paste and cook for a further 1 minute. Return the lamb to the pan, along with the grated tomato, stir and season with salt and pepper. Cover and simmer gently for 1¼ hours. After this time, set the lid slightly ajar so that the pan is partly covered and continue to simmer for 15 minutes, stirring occasionally, then take the lid off and simmer for 25 minutes, or until the sauce has thickened. When it is very thick, almost jam-like in consistency with the oil beginning to separate, stir in the honey and ground cinnamon and simmer for 2 minutes.

MELT the butter in a small frying pan, add the almonds and cook over medium heat, stirring occasionally, until the almonds are golden. Tip immediately onto a plate to prevent them from burning.

REMOVE the cinnamon stick from the lamb, transfer to a serving dish and sprinkle with the almonds. Serve with crusty bread or couscous.

Moroccans love their honey – this most ancient of sweeteners; it adds a special flavour to this tagine when combined with spices and tomatoes. The fried almonds add crunch.

BAHA

STEAMED LAMB WITH CUMIN

THIS IS A DISH OF SIMPLE BUT DELICIOUS FLAVOURS. WHEN SERVED AS PART OF A MOROCCAN MEAL, MORSELS OF LAMB ARE GENTLY PULLED FROM THE BONE WITH THE FINGERS. HOWEVER, LAMB CAN BE SLICED AND SERVED WITH BEETROOT AND CUMIN SALAD (PAGE 80) AND TINY BOILED POTATOES.

1.25 kg (2 lb 12 oz) lamb shoulder on the bone
1½ teaspoons ground cumin, plus extra to serve (optional)
1 teaspoon coarse salt, plus extra to serve (optional)
½ teaspoon freshly ground black pepper
pinch of ground saffron threads
6 garlic cloves, bruised
10–12 flat-leaf (Italian) parsley stalks
1 tablespoon olive oil

SERVES 4

TRIM the excess fat from the whole shoulder of lamb if necessary. Wipe the meat with damp paper towel and then cut small incisions into the meat on each side.

COMBINE the cumin, salt, black pepper and saffron and rub the mixture into the lamb, pushing it into the incisions. Cover and leave for 30 minutes for the flavours to penetrate. Place the lamb, fat side up, on a piece of muslin (cheesecloth), top with half the garlic cloves and tie the muslin over the top.

USING a large saucepan onto which a steamer will fit, or the base of a couscoussier, fill it three-quarters full with water. If using a saucepan and steamer, check that the base of the steamer is at least 3 cm (1¼ in) above the surface of the water. Cover and bring to the boil. Line the base of the steamer with the parsley stalks and the remaining garlic cloves. Place the lamb on top, put folded strips of foil around the rim of the steamer and put the lid on firmly to contain the steam. Keeping the heat just high enough to maintain a boil, steam for 2–2½ hours – do not lift the lid for the first 1½ hours of cooking. The lamb should easily pull away from the bone when cooked. Lift it out of the steamer and remove the muslin.

HEAT the oil in a large frying pan and quickly brown the lamb on each side for a more attractive presentation. This dish is traditionally served as part of a Moroccan meal, with the lamb taken from the bone with the fingers, accompanied with little dishes of coarse salt and ground cumin for extra seasoning.

Rub spices into the incisions of the lamb and then wrap in muslin (cheesecloth) to keep in the flavourings.

Preserved lemon is essential for this delicious dish. Cut rinsed rind into strips and add towards end of cooking.

TAGINE 'L'GHANMI BE JELBANA

LAMB TAGINE WITH PEAS AND LEMONS

PRESERVED LEMONS ADD A WONDERFUL FLAVOUR TO THIS DELICIOUS COMBINATION OF LAMB, GREEN PEAS, FRESH HERBS AND GROUND SPICES. WHILE SHELLED FRESH GREEN PEAS ARE PREFERRED, FROZEN PEAS ALSO GIVE GOOD RESULTS.

1 kg (2 lb 4 oz) boneless lamb shoulder or leg
2 tablespoons olive oil
1 brown onion, finely chopped
2 garlic cloves, finely chopped
1 teaspoon ground cumin
½ teaspoon ground ginger
½ teaspoon ground turmeric
3 tablespoons chopped coriander (cilantro) leaves
3 tablespoons chopped flat-leaf (Italian) parsley
1 teaspoon dried za'atar or 2 teaspoons chopped fresh lemon thyme
1½ preserved lemons (page 285)
235 g (8½ oz/1½ cups) shelled fresh or frozen green peas
2 teaspoons chopped mint
½ teaspoon caster (superfine) sugar

SERVES 4–6

TRIM the lamb and cut into 3 cm (1¼ in) pieces. Heat the olive oil in a large saucepan over high heat and brown the lamb in batches, removing to a dish when cooked. Add more oil if required.

REDUCE the heat to low, add the onion and cook for 5 minutes until softened. Add the garlic, cumin, ginger and turmeric and cook for a few seconds. Add 375 ml (13 fl oz/1½ cups) water and stir well to lift the browned juices off the base of the pan, then return the lamb to the pan with a little salt and a good grinding of black pepper. Add the coriander, parsley and za'atar, then cover and simmer over low heat for 1½ hours, or until the lamb is tender.

SEPARATE the preserved lemons into quarters and rinse well under cold running water, removing and discarding the pulp and membranes. Cut the rind into strips and add to the lamb, along with the peas, mint and sugar. Return to a simmer, cover and simmer for a further 10 minutes, or until the peas are cooked. Serve hot.

TAGINE 'L'GHANMI BEL BTATA WA ZITOUN

LAMB TAGINE WITH OLIVES AND POTATOES

SAFFRON PERFUMES THE POTATOES AND GIVES THEM A GOLDEN GLOW. IF YOU CAN PURCHASE CRACKED GREEN OLIVES, SO MUCH THE BETTER: BLANCH THEM FOR 2 MINUTES ONLY EACH TIME, AS THE BITTERNESS CAN BE REMOVED MORE READILY.

1 kg (2 lb 4 oz) boneless lamb
    shoulder
3 tablespoons olive oil
2 brown onions, finely chopped
2 garlic cloves, finely chopped
1 teaspoon ground cumin
½ teaspoon ground ginger
½ teaspoon paprika
3 tablespoons chopped coriander
    (cilantro) leaves
3 tablespoons chopped flat-leaf
    (Italian) parsley
175 g (6 oz/1 cup) green olives
750 g (1 lb 10 oz) all-purpose
    potatoes
⅛ teaspoon ground saffron threads
1 tablespoon olive oil, extra

SERVES 4–6

TRIM the lamb and cut into 3 cm (1¼ in) pieces. Heat half the olive oil in a large saucepan over high heat and brown the lamb on each side in batches, removing to a dish when cooked. Add a little more oil as required.

REDUCE the heat to low, add the remaining olive oil and cook the onion for 8 minutes, or until softened. Add the garlic, cumin and ginger and cook for a few seconds. Add 375 ml (13 fl oz/ 1½ cups) water and stir well to lift the browned juices off the base of the pan. Return the lamb to the pan, along with the paprika, ½ teaspoon salt and a good grinding of black pepper. Add the coriander and parsley, then cover and simmer over low heat for 1–1¼ hours.

MEANWHILE, put the olives in a small saucepan, cover with water, then bring to the boil and cook for 5 minutes. Drain and repeat once more to sweeten the flavour. Add the drained olives to the lamb, cover and cook for a further 15–30 minutes, or until the lamb is tender.

PEEL the potatoes and cut them into quarters. Put in a pan, cover with lightly salted water and add the saffron. Bring to the boil and cook for 10 minutes, or until tender. Drain and toss lightly with the extra olive oil.

TRANSFER the lamb and sauce to a serving dish, arrange the potatoes around the lamb and serve.

TAGINE 'L'GHANMI BEL BARKOUK

LAMB SHANK AND PRUNE TAGINE

THE ADDITION OF PRUNES GIVES THIS DISH A SWEET–SOUR FLAVOUR, REVEALING ITS PERSIAN ORIGINS. ANY STEWING CUT OF LAMB MAY BE USED, BUT LAMB SHANKS ARE DELICIOUS COOKED IN THIS WAY. ASK YOUR BUTCHER FOR FRENCHED (TRIMMED) SHANKS FOR A NEATER APPEARANCE.

1 tablespoon oil
30 g (1 oz) butter
4 lamb shanks
1 brown onion, chopped
⅛ teaspoon ground saffron threads
½ teaspoon ground ginger
2 cinnamon sticks
4 coriander (cilantro) sprigs, tied in a bunch
zest of ½ lemon, removed in wide strips
300 g (10½ oz/1⅓ cups) pitted prunes
2 tablespoons honey
1 tablespoon sesame seeds, toasted

SERVES 4

FRENCHED lamb shanks are trimmed of excess fat with the knuckle end of the bone sawn off. If unavailable, use whole shanks and ask the butcher to saw them in half for you.

PLACE a heavy-based saucepan over high heat, add the oil and butter, then add the lamb shanks. Brown the shanks on all sides and remove to a plate.

REDUCE the heat to medium, add the onion and cook gently for 5 minutes to soften. Add 375 ml (13 fl oz/1½ cups) water, the saffron, ginger, cinnamon sticks and coriander sprigs and season, to taste. Stir well and return the lamb shanks to the pan. Cover and simmer over low heat for 1 hour, then add the strips of lemon zest and cook for a further 30 minutes.

ADD the prunes and honey, cover and simmer for a further 30 minutes, or until the lamb is very tender. Remove and discard the coriander sprigs. Serve hot, sprinkled with sesame seeds.

A small bunch of coriander sprigs adds flavour without altering the colour of the delicious prune sauce. Remove before serving.

PICKLES Jars of pickled vegetables (left) grace the shelves of shops specialising in all types of pickles – turnips, onions and cauliflower – with the bottles containing a less fiery version of harissa. Preserved lemons and cured olives dominate such outlets (centre); glossy multi-coloured and green brine-cured olives contrast with the shrivelled, dry-cured black olives set before a dish of drained pickled onions.

PRESERVES

THE MOST FAMOUS OF MOROCCO'S PRESERVES IS HAMED MARKAD (PRESERVED LEMONS). THE TRANSFORMATION OF WHOLE LEMONS INTO A NEW INGREDIENT, UNIQUE IN TASTE AND SILKEN IN TEXTURE, IS ACHIEVED BY PRESERVING THEM WITH SALT, LEMON JUICE AND BOILED WATER. THEY ARE READY IN 4–6 WEEKS, THEIR CHARACTER TRANSFORMED.

While many Moroccans preserve their own, city dwellers prefer to buy preserved lemons from a vendor, either by the jar, or loose, according to immediate needs.

Olives are picked at various stages – green, half-ripe with a blush of red, uniformly red or black, resulting in cured olives of many hues and flavours. Some green olives are left whole or cracked to hasten the pickling process. Curing methods vary; for example, cracked olives are soaked in cold water for three days, with water changed daily, then cured in brine for several weeks until they lose their bitterness. For the tasty, shrivelled black olives, ripe olives are layered with salt in baskets and weighted. After five days they are spread out and sun-dried for a day, then the process is repeated twice

A bucket of preserved lemons (top left) in their briny, lemony liquid; these have obviously been preserved for some time as the liquid has taken on a typical amber hue. Spicy preserved meat (*khli'*) is piled in a bowl (bottom left), much sought after by city dwellers as many rural dwellers make their own from beef or lamb. Green and red-hued olives and pickles (right) are set out to tempt the local shoppers.

more. With an intense flavour, these are the most popular olives. A variety of vegetables are pickled in the Middle East manner, that is in brine and vinegar.

A popular preserve is *khli'*, a type of meat confit made by rural Moroccans. Many city dwellers take advantage of an important festival to make it. *Aid el kebhir* is such an occasion. It's a five-day festival of the sacrifice of the lamb (commemorating Abraham's sacrifice). Each household buys live lambs, often well before the festival. The lamb is ritually slaughtered by a family member or butcher on the first day, with lamb cuts, beginning with offal (fancy meats), cooked and consumed during this period. Any uncooked lamb not consumed during festivities is often preserved as *khli'*.

KSEKSOU BIDAWI

COUSCOUS WITH LAMB AND SEVEN VEGETABLES

THE NUMBER SEVEN IS CONSIDERED AUSPICIOUS, HENCE THE SEVEN VEGETABLES IN THIS POPULAR

DISH. THE CORRECT TRANSLATION OF 'BIDAWI' IS 'IN THE STYLE OF CASABLANCA' (DAR-EL-BEIDA IN

ARABIC). IN MOROCCAN HOUSEHOLDS, COUSCOUS IS SERVED ON FRIDAYS.

1 kg (2 lb 4 oz) lamb shoulder,
   boned
3 tablespoons olive oil
2 brown onions, quartered
2 garlic cloves, finely chopped
½ teaspoon ground turmeric
½ teaspoon paprika
¼ teaspoon ground saffron threads
1 cinnamon stick
4 coriander (cilantro) sprigs and
   4 flat-leaf (Italian) parsley sprigs,
   tied in a bunch
400 g (14 oz) tin chopped tomatoes
1½ teaspoons freshly ground black
   pepper
3 carrots, peeled and cut into thick
   sticks
3 small turnips, peeled and
   quartered
30 g (1 oz/¼ cup) raisins
4 zucchini (courgettes), cut into
   sticks
400 g (14 oz) firm pumpkin (winter
   squash) or butternut pumpkin
   (squash), peeled and cut into
   2.5 cm (1 in) chunks
420 g (15 oz) tin chickpeas, rinsed
   and drained
1 quantity couscous (page 278)
2–3 teaspoons harissa (page 286),
   to taste

SERVES 6–8

TRIM the lamb of excess fat if necessary, then cut into 2 cm (¾ in) cubes.

HEAT the oil in a large saucepan or the base of a large couscoussier and add the lamb, onion and garlic. Cook over medium heat, turning the lamb once, just until the lamb loses its red colour. Stir in the turmeric, paprika and saffron, add 750 ml (26 fl oz/3 cups) water, then add the cinnamon stick, the bunch of herbs, tomatoes, pepper and 1½ teaspoons salt, or to taste. Bring to a gentle boil, then cover and simmer over low heat for 1 hour. Add the carrots and turnips and cook for a further 20 minutes.

ADD the raisins, zucchini, pumpkin and chickpeas to the saucepan, adding a little water if necessary to almost cover the ingredients. Cook for a further 20 minutes, or until the meat and vegetables are tender.

WHILE the stew is cooking, prepare the couscous. Steam it either over the stew or over a saucepan of boiling water.

PILE the couscous in a deep, heated platter and make a dent in the centre. Remove the herbs and cinnamon stick from the stew and ladle the meat and vegetables into the hollow and on top of the couscous, letting some tumble down the sides. Moisten with a little broth from the stew. Pour 250 ml (9 fl oz/1 cup) of the remaining broth into a bowl and stir in the harissa. The harissa-flavoured broth is added to the couscous to keep it moist, and according to individual taste.

In Morocco, couscous comes in three different sized grains; medium or regular grains are preferred.

SLOW-COOKED BEEF WITH HERBS

TANGIA IS A BACHELOR'S DISH, NAMED FOR THE EARTHENWARE AMPHORA IN WHICH IT IS COOKED. INGREDIENTS ARE PLACED IN THE POT, THE TOP SEALED WITH PARCHMENT AND STRING, THEN TAKEN TO THE LOCAL BATHHOUSE FURNACE ROOM AND COOKED IN THE EMBERS FOR HOURS.

1 kg (2 lb 4 oz) chuck steak or
  boneless beef shin
1½ brown onions, finely chopped
4 garlic cloves, finely chopped
2 tablespoons olive oil
2 teaspoons ras el hanout
  (page 286)
½ teaspoon harissa (page 286), or
  to taste, or ⅛ teaspoon cayenne
  pepper
¼ teaspoon freshly ground black
  pepper
3 ripe tomatoes
1½ preserved lemons (page 285)
2 teaspoons honey
1 tablespoon chopped coriander
  (cilantro) leaves
2 tablespoons chopped flat-leaf
  (Italian) parsley

SERVES 4–6

TRIM the beef and cut into 2.5 cm (1 in) pieces. Place the beef in a deep casserole dish. Add the onion, garlic, oil, ras el hanout, harissa and the black pepper and season with salt. Toss the meat with the marinade. Preheat the oven to 140°C (275°F/Gas 1).

HALVE the tomatoes crossways and squeeze out the seeds. Coarsely grate the tomatoes down to the skins, grating them straight into the casserole. Discard the skins. Rinse the preserved lemons and remove the pulp and membranes. Chop the rind into chunks, reserving some for garnish, and add to the meat, along with the honey, coriander and 1 tablespoon of the parsley. Stir well, then cover and cook in the oven for 3½ hours. Juices from the meat should keep the dish moist, but check after 1½ hours of cooking and add a little water if necessary.

WHEN the meat is very tender, transfer to a serving dish, scatter over the reserved lemon rind and garnish with the remaining parsley.

TAGINE LAHM BIL MLOUKHIYA WAL MATISHA
BEEF TAGINE WITH OKRA AND TOMATOES

TO PREVENT THE OKRA FROM BREAKING UP DURING COOKING, COOKS PASS A NEEDLE AND THREAD

THROUGH THE CONICAL STEMS OF THE PODS, TYING THE THREAD TO FORM A 'NECKLACE'. WHEN THE

TAGINE HAS TO BE STIRRED OR REMOVED, THIS IS LIFTED WITH THE END OF A WOODEN SPOON.

1 kg (2 lb 4 oz) beef chuck steak
3 tablespoons olive oil
1 brown onion, finely chopped
3 garlic cloves, finely chopped
½ teaspoon ground cumin
½ teaspoon ground turmeric
400 g (14 oz) tin chopped, peeled
    tomatoes
½ teaspoon caster (superfine) sugar
1 cinnamon stick
2 tablespoons chopped flat-leaf
    (Italian) parsley
1 tablespoon chopped coriander
    (cilantro) leaves, plus extra leaves,
    to serve
500 g (1 lb 2 oz) small fresh okra

SERVES 4–6

TRIM the steak and cut into 2.5 cm (1 in) pieces. Heat half the olive oil in a large saucepan over medium heat and brown the beef in batches, adding a little more oil as needed. Set aside in a dish.

REDUCE the heat to low, add the onion and the remaining oil to the pan and cook gently for 10 minutes, or until softened. Add the garlic, cumin and turmeric, cook for a few seconds, then add the tomatoes, sugar, cinnamon stick, 1 teaspoon salt and a good grinding of black pepper. Return the beef to the pan, add the parsley, coriander and 250 ml (9 fl oz/1 cup) water. Cover the pan and simmer over low heat for 1½ hours, or until the meat is almost tender.

MEANWHILE, trim the very ends of the okra stems – do not cut into the pods. Rinse the okra in a colander under cold running water. Check that there is sufficient liquid in the saucepan, add a little more water if necessary so that the meat is almost covered, and place the okra on top. Lightly sprinkle with a little salt, cover and simmer for a further 30 minutes. Do not stir during this stage of cooking.

SCATTER with the extra coriander leaves and serve with crusty bread.

One wonders if it is the shape of the okra that appeals to Moroccans, or the taste. Certainly they make the most of its shape when presenting a cooked dish.

BEEF TAGINE WITH SWEET POTATOES

USE THE ORANGE-FLESHED SWEET POTATO AS IT IS MEALY AND SWEET, AND KEEPS ITS SHAPE WHEN COOKED. THE TAGINE IS FINISHED AND BROWNED IN THE OVEN; IN TRADITIONAL MOROCCAN COOKING, IT WOULD BE COVERED WITH A METAL LID WITH GLOWING CHARCOAL PLACED ON TOP.

1 kg (2 lb 4 oz) blade or chuck
   steak
3 tablespoons olive oil
1 brown onion, finely chopped
½ teaspoon cayenne pepper
½ teaspoon ground cumin
1 teaspoon ground turmeric
½ teaspoon ground ginger
2 teaspoons paprika
2 tablespoons chopped flat-leaf
   (Italian) parsley
2 tablespoons chopped coriander
   (cilantro) leaves
2 tomatoes
500 g (1 lb 2 oz) orange sweet
   potatoes

SERVES 4–6

TRIM the steak of any fat and cut into 2.5 cm (1 in) pieces. Heat half the oil in a saucepan and brown the beef in batches over high heat, adding a little more oil as needed. Set aside in a dish.

REDUCE the heat to low, add the onion and the remaining oil to the pan and gently cook for 10 minutes, or until the onion has softened. Add the cayenne pepper, cumin, turmeric, ginger and paprika, cook for a few seconds, then add 1 teaspoon salt and a good grinding of black pepper. Return the beef to the pan, along with the parsley, coriander and 250 ml (9 fl oz/1 cup) water. Cover and simmer over low heat for 1½ hours, or until the meat is almost tender.

PEEL the tomatoes. To do this, score a cross in the base of each one using a knife. Put the tomatoes in a bowl of boiling water for 20 seconds, then plunge into a bowl of cold water to cool. Remove from the water and peel the skin away from the cross – the skin should slip off easily. Slice the tomatoes. Peel the sweet potatoes, cut them into 2 cm (¾ in) chunks and leave in cold water until required, as this will prevent them discolouring. Preheat the oven to 180°C (350°F/Gas 4).

TRANSFER the meat and its sauce to an ovenproof serving dish (the base of a tagine would be ideal). Drain the sweet potatoes and spread them on top of the beef. Top with the sliced tomatoes. Cover with foil (or the lid of the tagine) and bake for 40 minutes. Remove the foil, increase the oven temperature to 220°C (425°F/Gas 7) and raise the dish to the upper oven shelf. Cook until the tomatoes and sweet potatoes are flecked with brown and are tender. Serve from the dish.

Put sweet potato slices in a bowl of cold water to prevent them discolouring until ready to add your cooking.

KEFTA TAGINE BIL BEID

MEATBALL TAGINE WITH TOMATO AND EGGS

FOR COMMUNAL EATING IN THE MOROCCAN MANNER, THIS DISH IS SERVED DIRECTLY AT THE TABLE IN THE DISH IN WHICH IT IS COOKED. WITH THE AID OF BREAD, DINERS MANAGE TO GET THEIR FAIR PORTION OF THE EGG. BREAD IS ALSO A MUST FOR MOPPING UP THE FULL-FLAVOURED SAUCE.

700 g (1 lb 9 oz) minced (ground) lamb
1 small brown onion, finely chopped
2 garlic cloves, finely chopped
2 tablespoons finely chopped flat-leaf (Italian) parsley
2 tablespoons finely chopped coriander (cilantro) leaves
½ teaspoon cayenne pepper
½ teaspoon ground ginger
1 teaspoon ground cumin
1 teaspoon paprika
2 tablespoons olive oil
4 eggs

SAUCE
2 tablespoons olive oil
1 brown onion, finely chopped
2 garlic cloves, finely chopped
2 teaspoons ground cumin
½ teaspoon ground cinnamon
1 teaspoon paprika
2 x 400 g (14 oz) tins chopped tomatoes
2 teaspoons harissa (page 286), or to taste
4 tablespoons chopped coriander (cilantro) leaves

SERVES 4

PUT the lamb, onion, garlic, herbs and spices in a bowl and mix well. Season with salt and pepper. Roll tablespoons of the mixture into balls.

HEAT the oil in a large frying pan over medium–high heat, add the meatballs in batches and cook for 8–10 minutes, or until browned all over, turning occasionally. Remove the meatballs and set them aside in a bowl. Wipe the frying pan with paper towel.

TO MAKE the sauce, heat the olive oil in the frying pan, add the onion and cook over medium heat for 5 minutes, or until the onion is soft. Add the garlic, cumin, cinnamon and paprika and cook for 1 minute, or until fragrant. Stir in the tomatoes and harissa and bring to the boil. Reduce the heat and simmer for 20 minutes.

ADD the meatballs, cover and simmer for 10 minutes, or until cooked. Stir in the coriander, then carefully break the eggs into the simmering tagine and cook until just set. Season and serve with crusty bread to mop up the juices.

After cooking the meatballs in the sauce, this can be transferred to the base of a tagine or other oven dish, and the eggs broken into it and cooked in a moderate oven until they've set to your taste.

FESTIVE FOOD

Using a mixture of green and black olives adds more appeal to these warm olives. Shred the lemon zest finely; however, if you have preserved lemon on hand, use strips of rind instead.

ZITOUN BIL HAMED

WARM OLIVES WITH LEMON AND HERBS

WHILE A CHOICE OF OLIVES IS GIVEN, A COMBINATION OF BOTH ADDS VARIETY IN COLOUR AND FLAVOUR. BOILING REDUCES SALT CONTENT AND 'SWEETENS' THE OLIVES. CRACKED GREEN OLIVES CAN BE DIFFICULT TO OBTAIN; IF GREEN OLIVES ARE USED, SICILIAN GREEN OLIVES ARE IDEAL.

350 g (12 oz/2 cups) cured cracked
  green or black Kalamata olives
80 ml (2½ fl oz/⅓ cup) olive oil
1 teaspoon fennel seeds
2 garlic cloves, finely chopped
pinch of cayenne pepper
finely shredded zest and juice of
  1 lemon
1 tablespoon finely chopped
  coriander (cilantro) leaves
1 tablespoon finely chopped flat-leaf
  (Italian) parsley

SERVES 4

RINSE the olives, drain and place in a saucepan with enough water to cover.

BRING to the boil and cook for 5 minutes, then drain in a sieve. Set aside. Add the olive oil and fennel seeds to the saucepan and heat gently until fragrant.

ADD the garlic, olives, cayenne pepper and the lemon zest and juice. Toss for 2 minutes, or until the olives are hot.

TRANSFER to a bowl and toss with the coriander and parsley. Serve hot with crusty bread to soak up the juices.

ZITOUN MESLALLA
MARINATED OLIVES

WHEREVER OLIVES ARE SOLD, MARINATED OLIVES ARE DISPLAYED ALONGSIDE THE GREEN AND BLACK VARIETIES, WITH A LITTLE MORE ADDED TO THE PRICE TAG FOR THE EXTRA INGREDIENTS. PREPARING THEM AT HOME IS SIMPLE, WITH DELICIOUS RESULTS.

PRESERVED LEMON OLIVES
½ preserved lemon (page 285)
½ teaspoon finely chopped red chilli
½ teaspoon ground cumin
2 tablespoons finely chopped
    coriander (cilantro) leaves
2 tablespoons finely chopped flat-
    leaf (Italian) parsley
2 garlic cloves, finely chopped
2 tablespoons lemon juice
125 ml (4 fl oz/½ cup) olive oil
500 g (1 lb 2 oz/3 cups) cured
    green olives (whole or cracked)

HARISSA OLIVES
1 red capsicum (pepper), or
    2 tablespoons chopped roasted
    red capsicum (pepper)
2 teaspoons harissa (page 286)
2 garlic cloves, finely chopped
125 ml (4 fl oz/½ cup) olive oil
500 g (1 lb 2 oz/2⅔ cups) black
    olives, such as kalamata

MAKES ABOUT 500 G (1 LB 2 OZ/
3 CUPS)

TO MAKE the preserved lemon olives, rinse the preserved lemon half under cold running water. Remove the pulp and membrane and rinse the rind. Drain and pat dry with paper towels. Chop the lemon rind very finely and put in a bowl, along with the chilli, cumin, coriander, parsley, garlic and lemon juice. Stir well and beat in the olive oil. Rinse the green olives under cold running water and drain thoroughly. Add to the preserved lemon marinade, toss and transfer to clean jars.

TO MAKE the harissa olives, first roast the capsicum. Cut it into quarters, removing the seeds and white membrane. Have the pieces as flat as possible and place them, skin side up, under a hot grill (broiler) and grill (broil) until the skin blisters and blackens. Turn and cook for 2–3 minutes on the fleshy side. Place the pieces in a plastic bag, tuck the end of the bag underneath and allow to steam for 15 minutes. Remove the blackened skin, rinse and drain the capsicum pieces, then pat dry with paper towels. Finely chop one of the pieces – you will need 2 tablespoons of chopped roasted capsicum. (Use the remaining roasted capsicum in salads.) In a bowl, combine the chopped capsicum with the harissa and garlic, then beat in the olive oil. Rinse the black olives under cold running water and drain thoroughly. Add to the harissa marinade, toss and transfer to clean jars.

SEAL the jars and refrigerate for 1–2 days before using. Bring the olives to room temperature 1 hour before serving. Use the preserved lemon olives within 5 days; the harissa olives within 10 days.

Ingredients of varied hues and flavours enhance these marinated olives; roasted red capsicum (pepper) is available at gourmet food stores.

FRIED PASTRIES WITH SEAFOOD

WHEN MAKING SMALL PASTRIES USING FILO, THE LESS THE PASTRY IS HANDLED THE BETTER. STACK THE SHEETS AND CUT THE STRIPS AS DIRECTED IN THE METHOD; A CRAFT KNIFE IS EXCELLENT FOR CUTTING THROUGH THE STACK. AVOID USING A DAMP TEA TOWEL AS IT CAN RUIN THE FILO.

FISH OR PRAWN FILLING
250 g (9 oz) boneless white fish fillets, or 200 g (7 oz) cooked prawns (shrimp), peeled and deveined
2 tablespoons finely chopped flat-leaf (Italian) parsley
1 tablespoon finely chopped spring onion (scallion)
1 garlic clove, crushed
½ teaspoon paprika
¼ teaspoon ground cumin
pinch of cayenne pepper
1 tablespoon lemon juice
1 tablespoon olive oil

6 sheets filo pastry
1 egg white, lightly beaten
oil, for deep-frying
3 tablespoons caster (superfine) sugar, to serve
⅛ teaspoon cayenne pepper, to serve
1 teaspoon ground cinnamon, to serve

MAKES 24

TO MAKE the fish or prawn filling, first poach the fish gently in lightly salted water, to cover, until the flesh flakes – about 4–5 minutes. Remove from the poaching liquid to a plate and cover closely with plastic wrap so that the surface does not dry as it cools. When cool, flake the fish and put it in a bowl. If using cooked prawns, cut them into small pieces. Put the fish or the prawns in a bowl, add the parsley, spring onion, garlic, paprika, cumin, cayenne pepper, lemon juice and olive oil and toss well to mix.

STACK the filo sheets on a cutting board, and with a ruler and sharp knife, measure and cut across the width of the pastry to give strips 12 cm (4½ in) wide and 28–30 cm (11¼–12 in) long. Stack the cut filo in the folds of a dry tea towel (dish towel) or cover with plastic wrap to prevent it from drying out.

TAKE a filo strip and, with the narrow end towards you, fold it in half across its width to make a strip 6 cm (2½ in) wide. Place a generous teaspoon of filling 2 cm (¾ in) in from the base of the strip, fold the end diagonally across the filling so that the base lines up with the side of the strip, forming a triangle. Fold straight up once, then fold diagonally to the opposite side. Continue folding until near the end of the strip, then brush the filo lightly with egg white and complete the fold. Place on a cloth-covered tray, seam side down. Cover with a tea towel until ready to fry, and cook within 10 minutes.

HEAT the oil to 180°C (350°F), or until a cube of bread dropped into the oil browns in 15 seconds. Add four pastries at a time and fry until golden, turning to brown evenly. Remove with a slotted spoon; drain on paper towel. Serve hot with a small bowl of sugar mixed with cayenne and cinnamon.

Fold the filled pastries into triangles. When such pastries are fried the filo is not buttered.

SHLADA HAMED BIL BESLA WAL MA'DANOUS
FRESH LEMON, ONION AND PARSLEY SALAD

IN MOROCCO THIS SALAD IS SERVED AT THE BEGINNING OF A MEAL. ITS MOUTH-TINGLING, REFRESHING FLAVOUR MAKES A DELICIOUS ACCOMPANIMENT TO SIMPLE CHARGRILLED FISH, PRAWNS OR CHICKEN. TRY IT ALSO WITH SWEET-TASTING FISH COOKED WITH DATES OR PRUNES.

6 lemons
1 small red onion
1 teaspoon caster (superfine) sugar
3 tablespoons chopped flat-leaf
   (Italian) parsley

SERVES 6–8

PEEL the lemons with a sharp knife, making sure that all the pith and fine membranes are removed, to expose the flesh. Cut the lemons into 1 cm (½ in) thick slices and remove the seeds. Dice the lemon slices and put them in a bowl.

HALVE the onion, then slice it thinly. Add to the lemons, along with the sugar, parsley and 1 teaspoon salt. Toss and set aside for 10 minutes.

JUST before serving, lightly sprinkle with freshly ground black pepper. Serve with fish or as a refreshing, tart contrast to tagines that contain fruit.

Peel lemons, removing all traces of pith, then slice and dice. For a less tart salad, use Meyer lemons.

ORANGE AND DATE SALAD

A SWEET–SOUR SALAD THAT USES TWO OF MOROCCO'S MOST PROLIFIC FRUITS. PALATE-CLEANSING, IT IS USUALLY SERVED AS AN APPETISER SALAD AT THE BEGINNING OF A MEAL. HOWEVER, IT CAN ALSO BE SERVED AS A DESSERT – OMIT THE MINT LEAVES AND DUST LIGHTLY WITH CINNAMON.

6 sweet oranges
2 teaspoons orange flower water
8 fresh dates, pitted and thinly
   sliced lengthways
90 g (3¼ oz/¾ cup) slivered
   almonds, lightly toasted
small mint leaves, to serve

SERVES 4–6

CUT off the tops and bases of the oranges. Cut the peel off with a sharp knife, removing all traces of pith and cutting through the outer membranes to expose the flesh. Holding the orange over a bowl to catch any juice, segment the oranges by cutting between the visible membranes. Remove the seeds and place the segments in the bowl. Squeeze the remains of the oranges over the bowl to extract all the juice.

ADD the orange flower water and stir gently to combine. Cover with plastic wrap and refrigerate until chilled.

PLACE the orange segments and the juice on a large flat dish and scatter the dates and almonds over the top. Sprinkle the mint leaves over the top. Serve chilled.

FENNEL AND OLIVE SALAD

2 fennel bulbs
125 g (4½ oz/¾ cup) black olives
2 tablespoons lemon juice
80 ml (2½ fl oz/⅓ cup) extra virgin
   olive oil
2 tablespoons finely chopped flat-
   leaf (Italian) parsley
1 teaspoon finely chopped, seeded
   red chilli, optional

SERVES 4

WASH the fennel bulbs and remove the outer layers if they are wilted or damaged. Cut off the stems and slice thinly across the bulb to the base, discarding the base.

PUT the sliced fennel in a shallow bowl and scatter the black olives on top. Beat the lemon juice with the olive oil in a jug. Season to taste and add the parsley.

IF DESIRED, add the chilli. Beat well and pour over the fennel and olives just before serving. Toss lightly.

FENNEL AND OLIVE SALAD

ORANGE AND DATE SALAD

THE TAGINE Terracotta tagines lined up for sale (above) at one of the many village potters is a familiar sight in Morocco. The *tagine slaoui* is a shallow glazed earthenware cooking pot that sits on a *majmar*, a charcoal brazier of unglazed earthenware. The lid is a distinctive conical shape with the top fashioned into a knob so that it can be easily removed with one hand.

TAGINES

BERBER INGENUITY CREATED THE TAGINE MANY CENTURIES AGO. BOTH THE POT, AND THE FOOD COOKED IN IT, ARE CALLED TAGINES. MADE OF EARTHENWARE, THEIR COLOUR IS DETERMINED BY THE CLAY AVAILABLE TO THE POTTERS. DESIGNS ARE OFTEN CUT INTO THE CLAY PRIOR TO FIRING.

The *tagine slaoui* can be small enough to cook a single serve or large enough to cook for a dozen or more. The dish for cooking is glazed, but lids are usually unglazed inside and colourfully designed and glazed on the outside, making them decorative without compromising function. During cooking, steam condenses inside the conical lid and drips back into the food to prevent it drying out. The knob on the lid is functional; as well as being easy to lift with one hand, while stirring the food with the other, its concave shape makes it an ideal spoon rest. Tagines are also used for storing bread, and the base can be used for serving fresh fruit. Note that for kitchens without a tagine, a baking dish is a good substitute.

In modern city kitchens, the food is often cooked in a saucepan or pressure cooker, then served in the tagine, especially if it is fully decorated and glazed. The shallowness of the base is deliberate, so that the food may be accessed easily when eating with the thumb and first two fingers of the right hand in the Moroccan manner. Etiquette dictates that the diner takes food from the section of the tagine that is in front of them. When entertaining, a host might move a tasty morsel to the section of the tagine facing the guest or guests.

A TRADITIONAL TAGINE A chermoula-type mix of herbs, onion and garlic is placed in the base of the tagine along with spices, seasoning and cooking oil. Chopped meat or chicken on the bone is added and the aromatic mixture is rubbed in, then left for a time. Some cooks prefer to cook the onion and garlic in the oil, adding herbs and spices; then the meat is added and turned in the mixture

Tagines lined up in a restaurant courtyard (above left), each simmering slowly over its charcoal brazier made of iron (*canoun*). In the courtyard of a house, a tagine is simmered on a *majmar* with a stirring spoon resting on top of the lid (centre); the cooked tagine (right) ready to be taken to the table – its lid will be replaced to retain the heat.

TO SEASON A TAGINE

Before using a tagine, it must be seasoned, or 'matured', otherwise it could crack when first used. This also serves to remove the earthenware flavour, especially of the unglazed interior of the lid. While this is usually done on a charcoal brazier, an oven is the better option. Check that the tagine fits in the oven, removing upper shelves. Preheat oven to 150ºC (300ºF/Gas 2). Wash the new tagine and lid, and wipe dry. To the tagine base, add one peeled, roughly chopped onion, 2 roughly chopped carrots, 2 whole garlic cloves, 1 bay leaf and 2–3 tablespoons olive oil. Almost fill with water. Cover and place in the preheated oven for 40 minutes. Remove and leave at room temperature to cool slowly. Discard contents, wash tagine in hot suds and dry thoroughly. When cooking in a tagine, it is better to use it over a medium–heat charcoal fire; if using a tagine on a gas fire or an electric hotplate, low heat and a good heat diffuser is recommended; however, tagines are excellent for oven cooking.

until it begins to stiffen and seal. Water is the final ingredient, and the tagine is cooked, covered, over a charcoal fire until the meat is almost tender. Vegetables are prepared and added according to the cooking time each requires. A tagine can take up to 2½ hours to cook until the meat is almost falling off the bones, so that it is easier to take apart with the fingers when eating.

SHLADA BIL KHIZOU WA LITCHINE

CARROT AND ORANGE SALAD

THE COMBINATION OF CARROT AND ORANGE IS NOT CONFINED TO MOROCCAN CUISINE. SOME COOKS JUICE THE ORANGES, SHRED THE CARROTS AND BLEND THESE TO A THICK PUREE WITH THE REMAINING INGREDIENTS. IT IS SIPPED FROM SMALL GLASSES.

3 sweet oranges
500 g (1 lb 2 oz) carrots
2 tablespoons lemon juice
1 teaspoon ground cinnamon, plus extra, to serve
1 tablespoon caster (superfine) sugar
1 tablespoon orange flower water
small mint leaves, to serve

SERVES 6

CUT off the tops and bases of the oranges. Cut the peel off using a sharp knife, removing all traces of pith and cutting through the outer membranes to expose the flesh. Holding the orange over a bowl to catch the juice, segment the oranges by cutting between the membranes. Remove the seeds and place the segments in the bowl. Squeeze the remains of the orange to extract all the juice. Pour the juice into another bowl.

PEEL and julienne the carrots using a sharp knife. Put the carrots in the bowl with the orange juice. Add the lemon juice, cinnamon, sugar, orange flower water and a small pinch of salt. Stir well to combine. Cover the carrot mixture and oranges and refrigerate until required.

JUST before serving, drain off the accumulated juice from the oranges and arrange the segments around the edge of a serving dish. Pile the julienned carrots in the centre and top with the mint leaves. Dust the oranges lightly with a little of the extra cinnamon.

Julienne the carrots with a sharp knife; better still, use a plastic mandolin (vegetable slicer) with a julienne blade, or a special julienne shredder.

ZAALOOK

WARM EGGPLANT SALAD

THIS CHUNKY COOKED SALAD MAKES A PERFECT STARTER WITH CRUSTY BREAD. IF YOUR EGGPLANTS ARE GLOSSY, HEAVY FOR THEIR SIZE AND YIELD SLIGHTLY WHEN PRESSED, THESE ARE SIGNS THAT THEY ARE NOT OVER-RIPE. IN THIS CASE, YOU CAN OMIT THE SALTING AS THEY ARE LESS BITTER.

2 x 450 g (1 lb) eggplants
(aubergines)
3 tomatoes
olive oil, for frying
2 garlic cloves, finely chopped
1 teaspoon paprika
½ teaspoon ground cumin
¼ teaspoon cayenne pepper, or to taste
2 tablespoons finely chopped coriander (cilantro) leaves
2½ tablespoons lemon juice
½ preserved lemon (page 285) (optional) or fresh lemon slices, to serve

SERVES 6–8

USING a vegetable peeler, remove 1 cm (½ in) wide strips of skin along the length of each eggplant. Cut the eggplants into 1 cm (½ in) slices, sprinkle with salt and layer the slices in a colander. Leave for 20–30 minutes, then rinse under cold running water. Drain, squeeze the slices gently, then pat them dry with paper towel.

PEEL the tomatoes by first scoring a cross in the base of each one using a knife. Put in a bowl of boiling water for 20 seconds, then plunge into a bowl of cold water to cool. Remove from the water and peel the skin away from the cross – it should slip off easily. Cut the tomatoes in half crossways and squeeze out the seeds. Chop the tomatoes and set aside.

HEAT the olive oil in a frying pan to a depth of 5 mm (¼ in). Fry the eggplant slices in batches until browned on each side and set aside on a plate. Add more oil to the pan as needed.

USING the oil left in the pan, cook the garlic over low heat for a few seconds. Add the tomatoes, paprika, cumin and cayenne pepper and increase the heat to medium. Add the eggplant slices and cook, mashing the eggplant and tomato gently with a fork. Continue to cook until most of the liquid has evaporated. When the oil separates, drain off some if it seems excessive; however, some oil should be left in as it adds to the flavour of the dish. Add the coriander and lemon juice and season with freshly ground black pepper and a little salt if necessary. Transfer to a serving bowl.

IF USING preserved lemon, rinse under cold running water and remove the pulp and membranes. Chop the rind into small pieces and scatter over the eggplant or, alternatively, garnish with slices of fresh lemon. Serve warm or at room temperature with bread.

By peeling strips of skin from the eggplants, they break up more easily, with no long pieces of skin in the salad. Mash the ingredients just enough so that they combine but still remain chunky in texture.

COQUE BIL FUL

ARTICHOKES WITH BROAD BEANS

GLOBE ARTICHOKES AND BROAD BEANS APPEAR IN THE SOUKS AT THE SAME TIME, BUT THE BEANS ARE AT THEIR BEST EARLY IN THE SEASON. MATURE BROAD BEANS SHOULD BE SKINNED BEFORE COOKING – BLANCH, COOL, PEEL. WATERCRESS SUBSTITUTES FOR A WILD HERB CALLED BAKOOLA.

1 lemon
4 globe artichokes
3 tablespoons olive oil
1 white onion, finely chopped
2 garlic cloves, finely chopped
2 tablespoons chopped flat-leaf (Italian) parsley
2 tablespoons chopped fresh fennel leaves
1 kg (2 lb 4 oz) fresh broad (fava) beans, shelled
3 large handfuls cleaned watercress
1 preserved lemon (page 285)
fennel sprigs, or chopped fennel, to serve

SERVES 4–6

HALVE the lemon and add juice of one half to a bowl of cold water. Cut remainder of the lemon in half and use to rub cut surfaces as artichokes are prepared.

CUT stem off artichoke close to base, and cut a 12 cm (4½ in) piece from the top of the stem, discarding remainder. Pull off and discard 4–5 layers of outer leaves of artichoke until the base of the remaining leaves are light yellow–green. Trim carefully around base where leaves were removed. Each time you make a new cut or trim, rub the exposed surface with cut lemon. Cut and discard top quarter of artichoke, cut in half, remove hairy choke with a teaspoon, and cut again to make quarters. Drop into the lemon water. Peel the fibrous layer from the stem, cut across in half and add to bowl. Repeat until all are prepared.

IN A large stainless steel or enamelled saucepan, warm the oil over medium heat. Add the onion and cook gently until soft, about 5 minutes. Add garlic, cook a few seconds, then stir in herbs and drained artichokes and stems. Cook for 2 minutes, then add fresh broad beans and 750 ml (26 fl oz/3 cups) water. Season and bring to the boil over high heat then reduce to low–medium and simmer, partly covered, for 15 minutes.

MEANWHILE chop watercress coarsely. Remove flesh from preserved lemon and discard. Rinse the rind well, cut into strips and set aside a quarter of them for garnish. Stir watercress and remaining preserved lemon strips into artichokes and continue to cook, uncovered, for a further 10–15 minutes until artichokes and beans are tender. Boil rapidly towards end of cooking to reduce so that only half the liquid remains. Transfer to a shallow serving dish and sprinkle top with reserved lemon strips and fennel leaves. Serve with bread.

Cut tops off artichokes, halve and remove the hairy choke and prickly inner leaves with a spoon.

MEZGHALDI B'BESLA BIL BOUDENJAL

CARAMELISED ONIONS WITH CHARGRILLED EGGPLANTS

THESE SPICY, CARAMELISED ONIONS ARE USUALLY SERVED ON THEIR OWN AS AN APPETISER SALAD, BUT CAN ALSO BE TEAMED WITH CHARGRILLED EGGPLANT (AUBERGINE). THIS ALSO MAKES A DELICIOUS ACCOMPANIMENT TO CHARGRILLED MEATS OR CHICKEN.

4 brown onions
100 ml (3½ fl oz) olive oil
¼ teaspoon ground saffron threads
1 teaspoon ground ginger
1 teaspoon ground cinnamon
½ teaspoon allspice
1½ tablespoons honey
600 g (1 lb 5 oz) long thin eggplants
 (aubergines)

SERVES 4

HALVE the onions lengthways and cut them into slender wedges. Put them in a frying pan, cover with cold water and bring to the boil. Cover and simmer for 5 minutes. Drain the onion in a colander.

ADD 2 tablespoons of the olive oil to the pan and, over low heat, stir in the saffron, ginger, cinnamon and allspice. Cook for 1 minute, then increase the heat to medium and return the onion to the pan. Add the honey and 375 ml (13 fl oz/ 1½ cups) water and season with salt and freshly ground black pepper. Stir well, reduce the heat to low, cover and simmer for 40 minutes, then uncover and simmer for 10 minutes, or until most of the liquid has evaporated.

WASH and dry the eggplants. Leaving the green stalks on for effect, halve them lengthways. Using the remaining oil, brush all the eggplant halves on each side. Cook the eggplants in a heated chargrill pan or on a barbecue grill for 3–4 minutes each side until they are tender, adjusting the heat so they do not burn.

ARRANGE the eggplants, cut side up, on a platter or on individual plates and season lightly with salt. Top with the onion and pour over any juices from the pan. Serve hot or warm with crusty bread, or as an accompaniment to chicken or chargrilled meats.

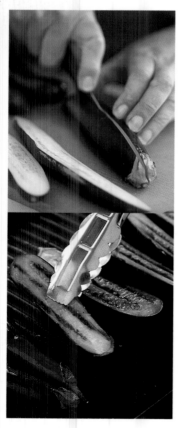

Select the more slender long eggplants so that they are not too thick when halved lengthways.

GAR'A HAMRA
PUMPKIN PURÉE

A BERBER SPECIALTY OF THE MIDDLE ATLAS, THIS IS MADE ON THE FIRST DAY AFTER RAMADAN AND SERVED WITH A CHICKEN TAGINE. THE PUMPKIN IS USUALLY BOILED, THEN FRIED, BUT AS SOME PUMPKINS CAN BECOME MUSHY VERY QUICKLY, USE THE FOLLOWING METHOD TO PREVENT THIS.

750 g (1 lb 10 oz) firm pumpkin (winter squash) or butternut pumpkin (squash)
2 tablespoons vegetable oil
¾ teaspoon ras el hanout (page 286)
1 tablespoon lemon juice
½ teaspoon lemon zest, finely chopped
1–2 tablespoons honey
2 teaspoons toasted sesame seeds

SERVES 4–6

PEEL and remove the seeds from the pumpkin and cut into 2 cm (¾ in) cubes. Put the pumpkin in a roasting tin with 2 tablespoons oil and toss to coat.

COMBINE the zest and juice and pour over the pumpkin. Sprinkle with the ras el hanout, season and drizzle with honey.

ROAST in a preheated 200°C (400°F/Gas 6) oven for 35 minutes, tossing occasionally with a spatula. Mash to a purée in the dish. Sprinkle with sesame seeds and serve warm.

GAR'A SHLADA BIL HAMED MARKAD
WARM PUMPKIN SALAD WITH PRESERVED LEMON

THE COMBINATION OF SWEET-TASTING PUMPKIN AND TART PRESERVED LEMON, HERBED AND SPICED IN THE MOROCCAN MANNER, ILLUSTRATES THE INGENUITY OF MOROCCAN COOKS. SERVE IN THE TRADITIONAL WAY BEFORE THE MAIN MEAL, OR AS AN ACCOMPANIMENT TO SIMPLY COOKED CHICKEN.

1 kg (2 lb 4 oz) firm pumpkin (winter squash) or butternut pumpkin (squash)
1 preserved lemon (page 285)
3 tablespoons olive oil
1 brown onion, grated
½ teaspoon ground ginger
½ teaspoon ground cumin
1 teaspoon paprika
2 tablespoons chopped flat-leaf (Italian) parsley
2 tablespoons chopped coriander (cilantro) leaves
1 tablespoon lemon juice

SERVES 4

PEEL pumpkin, remove seeds and cut into 2 cm (¾ in) chunks. Set aside. Remove pulp from preserved lemon, rinse rind, dice and set aside.

IN A large, lidded frying pan, heat olive oil on medium heat and add onion. Cook for 3 minutes, stir in ginger, cumin and paprika and cook for a further 30 seconds. Add pumpkin, parsley, coriander, lemon juice, the preserved lemon and 125 ml (4½ fl oz/½ cup) water. Season to taste, cover and simmer on low heat for 20 minutes until tender, tossing occasionally with a spatula, adding a little more water if necessary. Serve warm as an appetiser or hot as a vegetable accompaniment.

WARM PUMPKIN SALAD WITH PRESERVED LEMON

DJEJ 'MSHERMEL

CHICKEN WITH PRESERVED LEMON AND OLIVES

ONE OF THE CLASSIC DISHES OF MOROCCO, THIS COMBINATION OF SUBTLY SPICED CHICKEN, PRESERVED LEMON AND OLIVES IS USUALLY SERVED AT BANQUETS. USE UNPITTED GREEN OLIVES; IF BITTER, BLANCH THEM IN BOILING WATER FOR 5 MINUTES BEFORE ADDING TO THE CHICKEN.

¼ preserved lemon (page 285)
3 tablespoons olive oil
1.6 kg (3 lb 8 oz) chicken
1 brown onion, chopped
2 garlic cloves, chopped
625 ml (21½ fl oz/2½ cups)
   chicken stock
½ teaspoon ground ginger
1½ teaspoons ground cinnamon
pinch of saffron threads
100 g (3½ oz/½ cup) green olives
2 bay leaves
2 chicken livers
3 tablespoons chopped coriander
   (cilantro) leaves

SERVES 4

RINSE the preserved lemon quarter under cold running water, remove and discard the pulp and membranes. Drain the rind, pat dry with paper towel and cut into strips. Set aside.

PREHEAT the oven to 180°C (350°F/Gas 4). Heat 2 tablespoons of the olive oil in a large frying pan, add the chicken and brown on all sides. Place in a deep baking dish.

HEAT the remaining oil in the pan over medium heat, add the onion and garlic and cook for 5 minutes, or until the onion has softened. Add the chicken stock, ginger, cinnamon, saffron, olives, bay leaves and preserved lemon strips. Stir well, then pour the sauce around the chicken in the dish. Bake for 1½ hours, or until cooked through, adding a little more water or stock if the sauce gets too dry. Baste the chicken during cooking.

REMOVE the chicken from the dish, cover with foil and leave to rest. Pour the contents of the baking dish into a frying pan and place over medium heat. Add the chicken livers and mash them into the sauce as they cook. Cook for 5–6 minutes, or until the sauce has reduced and thickened. Add the chopped coriander. Cut the chicken into pieces and serve with the sauce.

Brown the chicken in a non-stick frying pan so that the chicken skin remains intact. Use the same pan for completing the sauce after chicken is cooked.

DJEJ BIL KSEKSOU

ROAST CHICKEN WITH COUSCOUS STUFFING

MOROCCAN COOKS USUALLY STEAM STUFFED CHICKEN OR COOK IT WHOLE IN A TAGINE. TO BROWN IT, THEY REMOVE IT FROM ITS SAUCE IF NECESSARY, AND FRY IT ON ALL SIDES IN A FRYING PAN. THE FOLLOWING RECIPE IS FOR OVEN-ROASTED CHICKEN.

1.6 kg (3 lb 8 oz) chicken
2 teaspoons paprika
30 g (1 oz) butter, softened
250 ml (9 fl oz/1 cup) chicken stock

STUFFING
140 g (5 oz/¾ cup) couscous
40 g (1½ oz/⅓ cup) raisins
30 g (1 oz) butter, diced
1 tablespoon honey
½ teaspoon ground cinnamon
40 g (1½ oz/¼ cup) blanched
   almonds, lightly toasted

SERVES 4–6

PREHEAT the oven to 180°C (350°F/Gas 4). Rinse the cavity of the chicken and dry with paper towel. Season the chicken on the outside and sprinkle with paprika. Rub it into the skin.

TO PREPARE the stuffing, put the couscous in a glass or ceramic lidded casserole dish and mix in the raisins, butter, honey and cinnamon. Pour on 125 ml (4 fl oz/½ cup) boiling water, stir well and set aside until the water has been absorbed. Fluff up the grains with a fork to break up the lumps, cover and microwave on full power for 2½ minutes. Fluff up again with the fork, add the almonds and toss through. Alternatively, follow the directions on the packet to prepare the couscous, adding the extra ingredients.

SPOON the stuffing into the cavity of the chicken, packing it in loosely. Tie the legs together and tuck the wing tips under. Reserve left-over stuffing.

SPREAD a little of the softened butter in the base of a roasting tin. Put the chicken, breast side up, in the tin, spread with the remaining butter and pour the stock into the tin. Roast for 1½–1¾ hours, basting often with the liquid in the pan. Remove to a platter, cover lightly with foil and rest in a warm place for 15 minutes before carving. The juices left in the roasting tin may be strained over the chicken. Reheat remaining couscous stuffing and serve with the chicken.

Rub salt and paprika onto the chicken and truss after stuffing. Rest cooked chicken before carving.

Besides giving chicken a good shape, tying the legs keeps in the stuffing. Use foil around the steamer to prevent steam escaping.

DJEJ MAFOOAR BIL ROZZ

STEAMED CHICKEN WITH RICE STUFFING

STEAMED CHICKEN IS USUALLY STUFFED WITH HOME-MADE NOODLES CALLED SHERIYA, HOWEVER THE FOLLOWING USES A RICE STUFFING FROM THE SPANISH-INFLUENCED NORTH. THE CHICKEN IS STEAMED TO MELTING TENDERNESS SO THAT THE MEAT CAN BE REMOVED EASILY WITH THE FINGERS.

1.5 kg (3 lb 5 oz) free-range chicken
2 bay leaves
3–4 parsley stalks
2 garlic cloves, unpeeled and
  bruised
1 tablespoon cumin seeds
1 tablespoon butter, or smen
  (page 282)

RICE STUFFING
115 g (4 oz/½ cup) short-grain rice
2 tablespoons olive oil
1 brown onion, chopped
2 tomatoes, peeled, seeded and
  chopped
2 tablespoons chopped flat-leaf
  (Italian) parsley
2 teaspoons chopped fresh mint
½ teaspoon paprika
pinch of cayenne pepper
185 ml (6 fl oz/¾ cup) chicken
  stock
1 tablespoon salt mixed with
  2 teaspoons ground cumin, to
  serve

SERVES 4–6

RINSE the cavity of the chicken and dry with paper towel. Rub salt onto the chicken.

TO PREPARE the stuffing, rinse rice in a sieve until water runs clear. Leave to drain. Put oil and onion in a saucepan and cook over medium heat for 5 minutes. Add rice and cook, stirring for 2 minutes, until it is opaque. Stir in tomatoes, parsley, mint, paprika, cayenne pepper and the chicken stock and bring to the boil. Cover and simmer on low heat for 8 minutes until liquid is absorbed. When cooled slightly, spoon stuffing loosely into the cavity of the chicken and tie the legs together. Refrigerate remaining stuffing in a covered bowl.

USING a large saucepan onto which a steamer will fit, fill it three-quarters full with water and add bay leaves. Check that the steamer base does not touch the water. Bring to the boil. Line base of steamer with parsley stalks and garlic cloves and place chicken on top. Cover chicken with a folded piece of muslin (cheesecloth). Put folded strips of foil around the saucepan rim, put steamer with chicken on top and press down so that the foil prevents steam escaping. Cover steamer tightly with lid.

KEEP heat just high enough to maintain boiling point and steam for 1½ hours. Do not lift lid for first 1 hour of cooking. After 1¼ hours, place remaining rice stuffing on a square of greased foil and position next to the chicken. Steam for a further 20 minutes and check if cooked – the leg and thigh moves freely when pushed forward. Lift onto a serving plate and put extra rice stuffing on one side. Toast cumin seeds in a dry pan until fragrant, add butter to pan and when melted, immediately pour over chicken. Serve with little bowls of the salt and cumin mix for extra seasoning.

TAGINE DJEJ BIL MACHMACH

CHICKEN TAGINE WITH APRICOTS

WHOLE CHICKEN OR CHICKEN CUT INTO PORTIONS IS USUAL IN MOROCCO. HOWEVER, CHICKEN BREASTS, OFF THE BONE AND WITH THE SKIN REMOVED, ARE USED IN THIS DISH TO DECREASE THE COOKING TIME. WHEN APRICOTS ARE NOT IN SEASON, TINNED APRICOTS ARE A GOOD ALTERNATIVE.

4 x 175 g (6 oz) skinless, boneless chicken breasts
40 g (1½ oz) butter
1 teaspoon ground cinnamon
1 teaspoon ground ginger
¼ teaspoon freshly ground black pepper
⅛ teaspoon cayenne pepper
1 brown onion, sliced
250 ml (9 fl oz/1 cup) chicken stock
6 coriander (cilantro) sprigs, tied in a bunch, plus extra to garnish
500 g (1 lb 2 oz) fresh apricots or 425 g (15 oz) tin apricot halves, in natural juice
2 tablespoons honey
1 quantity couscous (page 278)
2 tablespoons slivered almonds, toasted

SERVES 4

TRIM the chicken breasts of any fat or gristle. Melt the butter in a large frying pan. Add the spices and stir over low heat for 1 minute. Increase the heat to medium and add the chicken breasts. Turn them in the spiced butter and cook for 1 minute each side, without allowing the spices to burn.

ADD the onion to the pan around the chicken and cook for 5 minutes, stirring the onion and turning the chicken occasionally. Add the chicken stock and coriander sprigs and season if necessary. Reduce the heat to low, cover and simmer for 5 minutes, turning the chicken once.

WASH and halve the apricots and remove the stones. Place them, cut side down, around the chicken and drizzle with honey. Cover and simmer for 7–8 minutes, turning the apricots after 5 minutes. Remove the chicken to a plate, cover and rest for 2–3 minutes. Slice each breast on the diagonal.

PREPARE the couscous as directed. Put the hot couscous on serving plates and top each with some sliced chicken. Remove the coriander sprigs from the sauce and spoon the sauce and apricots over the chicken. Scatter with the almonds and extra coriander and serve hot.

Brown the chicken breast fillets in the hot, spiced butter. Fresh apricots are turned only once in the sauce towards the end of cooking, to keep them intact.

Heat the butter and *ras el hanout* until fragrant before adding the chicken; do not allow the spices to burn. The spices complement the prunes.

DJEJ BIL RAS EL HANOUT WA BARKOUK
SPICED CHICKEN WITH PRUNES

THE SPECIAL MOROCCAN SPICE MIX, RAS EL HANOUT, TOGETHER WITH ROSEWATER, ADDS FRAGRANCE TO THIS DISH OF CHICKEN AND PRUNES. WITH MODERN PROCESSING, PRUNES DO NOT REQUIRE PRE-SOAKING; USE PITTED PRUNES RATHER THAN HAVING TO PIT THEM YOURSELF – A STICKY TASK.

30 g (1 oz) butter
1½ teaspoons ras el hanout
  (page 286)
4 x 175 g (6 oz) chicken breast
  fillets
1 brown onion, sliced
250 ml (9 fl oz/1 cup) chicken stock
150 g (5½ oz/⅔ cup) pitted prunes
3 teaspoons honey
3 teaspoons lemon juice
3 teaspoons rosewater
couscous, to serve (page 278)

SERVES 4

MELT the butter in a large, lidded frying pan. Add the ras el hanout and stir over low heat for 30 seconds. Increase the heat to medium, add the chicken breast fillets and cook for 1 minute on each side, without allowing the spices to burn. Remove the chicken from the pan.

ADD the onion to the pan and cook over medium heat for 5 minutes or until softened. Pour in the chicken stock and add pitted prunes, honey, lemon juice and rosewater. Cover and simmer over low heat for 10 minutes.

RETURN the chicken to the pan, cover and simmer gently for 15 minutes or until chicken is just cooked through and tender. Slice the chicken breasts on the diagonal and serve with the prune sauce and steamed couscous.

MECHOUI
SLOW-ROASTED LAMB WITH CUMIN

THIS VERSION OF MECHOUI (WHOLE, SLOW-ROASTED LAMB) USES LAMB LEG; A FOREQUARTER OF
LAMB CAN BE PREPARED IN THE SAME WAY. WHILE INITIAL HEAT IS HIGH, THE LAMB SHOULD BE
COOKED IN A SLOW OVEN AND BASTED FREQUENTLY TO REMAIN MOIST.

2.25 kg (5 lb) leg of lamb
70 g (2½ oz) butter, softened at
   room temperature
3 garlic cloves, crushed
2 teaspoons ground cumin
3 teaspoons ground coriander
1 teaspoon paprika
1 tablespoon ground cumin, extra,
   to serve
1½ teaspoons coarse salt, to serve

SERVES 6

PREHEAT the oven to 220°C (425°F/Gas 7). With
a small sharp knife, cut small deep slits in the top
and sides of the lamb.

MIX the butter, garlic, spices and ¼ teaspoon salt
in a bowl to form a smooth paste. With the back
of a spoon, rub the paste all over the lamb, then
use your fingers to spread the paste evenly,
making sure all the lamb is covered.

PUT the lamb, bone side down, in a deep roasting
tin and place on the top shelf of the oven. Bake for
10 minutes, then baste with the pan juices and
return it to the centre shelf of the oven. Reduce
the oven temperature to 160°C (315°F/Gas 2–3).
Bake for 3¼ hours, basting every 20–30 minutes,
to ensure the lamb stays tender and flavoursome.
Carve the lamb into chunky pieces. Mix the extra
cumin with the coarse salt and serve on the side
for sprinkling over.

Make deep incisions in the lamb
so that the butter and spice mix
penetrates into the meat.

A DESERT STAPLE Plates of dates (top left) on display at a stand that sells *harira* (lamb and chickpea soup) – these are a traditional accompaniment to this soup. Two of the many varieties of dates on sale at a souk (bottom left), where cooking and table dates are stocked. Date palms (right) flourish outside the ancient walls of Marrakesh, situated in an area ideal for date growing.

DATES

ACCORDING TO A MOROCCAN SAYING, DATE PALMS MUST HAVE THEIR HEADS IN FIRE AND THEIR FEET IN WATER – THE HOT MOROCCAN SUN TO BRING THE FRUIT TO SUCCULENT SWEETNESS, AND GROUNDWATER FOR THEIR ROOTS TO MAINTAIN GROWTH. DATE PALMS, GROWING IN OASES, HAVE SUSTAINED NOMADIC TRIBES FOR MILLENNIA.

The date palm still sustains those who have not given up their traditional existence, and is equally as important to villagers and city dwellers. For food on the move, the date is difficult to beat – it provides an instant boost of energy with its high sugar content, with the bonus of a little protein, vitamins and minerals thrown in. The prophet Mohammed is said to have recommended dates with milk to break the daily fast during Ramadan, a practice still maintained by many Moroccans; however, the favoured 'break fast' meal at sundown is *harira* soup, fortified with chickpeas and soup noodles and served with dates and sweet, honeyed pastries. Dates are often used in tagines and as a stuffing for whole fish, and are also made into sweetmeats. Fresh dates take a year to mature, making their appearance in the

Dried fruit and nuts (above) on display at a souk. Besides stocking date varieties, there are raisins, apricots and prunes for cooking and snacking, dried banana slices, almonds, cashew nuts, peanuts in the shell, pumpkin seeds and flattened, dried figs strung on dried date-palm fronds. Besides being a source for stocking the home pantry, such stalls are heaven for health-conscious snackers.

souks in December, often arranged painstakingly in mini pyramids. Hues vary from light golden brown, through red-brown to a rich chocolate.

As well as its fruit, the date palm provides fronds, which are dried and used for baskets, table mats and as string; the fibre from its bark is made into ropes; the stones of the fruit are used for fuel; and the trunk provides timber. Date palms can produce fruit for 60 years; however, they can exceed 30 metres (100 feet) in height and are cut down when harvesting becomes too difficult. In the Erfoud oasis alone, one million date palms flourish, encompassing 30 varieties. The average annual yield is about 45 kg (100 lb) of fruit per tree. Muslims regard the date palm as the tree of life – it is easy to see why.

LAMB TAGINE WITH DATES

IN THIS RICH AND LUSCIOUS DISH, THE DRIED DATES ARE PITTED, AND ARE USED TO THICKEN THE SAUCE, WHICH CARRIES THEIR FLAVOUR THROUGH THE DISH. THE WHOLE DATES USED TO COMPLETE THE DISH ARE LEFT UNPITTED, OTHERWISE THEY CAN DISINTEGRATE.

1 kg (2 lb 4 oz) boneless lamb from shoulder or leg
30 g (1 oz) butter
1 brown onion, finely chopped
1 teaspoon ground ginger
1 teaspoon ground cinnamon
½ teaspoon freshly ground black pepper
55 g (2 oz/⅓ cup) pitted, chopped dried dates
pinch of ground saffron threads
2 tablespoons honey
2 tablespoons lemon juice
200 g (7 oz/1¼ cup) fresh or dessert dates (unpitted)
½ preserved lemon (page 285)
15 g (½ oz) butter, extra
40 g (1½ oz/⅓ cup) slivered almonds

SERVES 6

TRIM the lamb and cut into 2.5 cm (1 in) cubes. In a large heavy-based saucepan, melt the butter over low heat, add the onion and cook gently for 8 minutes. Sprinkle in the ginger, cinnamon and black pepper and stir for 1 minute. Increase the heat to high, add the lamb and stir until the colour of the meat changes. Reduce the heat, add 375 ml (13 fl oz/1½ cups) water, the chopped dates, saffron and 1 teaspoon salt. Reduce the heat to low, cover and simmer for 1½ hours, stirring occasionally to prevent the sauce sticking as the chopped dates cook to a purée.

STIR in the honey and lemon juice and adjust the seasoning. Put the unpitted dates on top, cover and simmer for 10 minutes, or until the dates are plump.

MEANWHILE, rinse the preserved lemon half under cold running water, remove and discard the pulp and membranes. Drain the rind, pat dry with paper towel and cut into strips. Melt the extra butter in a small frying pan over medium heat, add the almonds and brown lightly, stirring often, for 5 minutes. Tip immediately onto a plate to prevent over-browning.

REMOVE the whole dates from the top of the lamb and set them aside with the almonds. Ladle the meat into a serving dish or tagine and scatter the dates on top, along with the lemon strips and toasted almonds. Serve hot.

Stir lamb in onion–spice mix. Whole dates are placed on top of the meat so that they remain intact.

TAFAYA

LAMB WITH EGGS AND ALMONDS

TAFAYA IS SERVED AT CELEBRATIONS THROUGHOUT MOROCCO. TO GIVE THE DISH A FESTIVE TOUCH, SOME COOKS DIP THE SHELLED, BOILED EGGS IN SAFFRON-INFUSED HOT WATER, WHICH COLOURS THEM AND GIVES THEM A SPECIAL FRAGRANCE AND FLAVOUR.

1.25 kg (2 lb 12 oz) lamb shoulder
    chops
3 tablespoons olive oil
2 brown onions, coarsely grated
3 garlic cloves, finely chopped
2 teaspoons ground ginger
⅛ teaspoon ground saffron threads
3 tablespoons chopped coriander
    (cilantro) leaves
40 g (1½ oz) butter
150 g (5½ oz/1 cup) blanched
    almonds
6 hard-boiled eggs
coriander (cilantro) leaves, extra, to
    serve

SERVES 6

TRIM the excess fat from the chops. Heat half the olive oil in a large saucepan over high heat and brown the chops on each side in batches, removing to a dish when cooked. Add a little more oil as required.

REDUCE the heat to low, add the remaining oil and the onion and cook for 8 minutes, or until softened. Add the garlic and ginger and cook for a few seconds. Pour in 375 ml (13 fl oz/1½ cups) water and stir to lift the browned juices off the base of the pan. Return the lamb to the pan, along with the saffron, 1 teaspoon salt and a good grinding of black pepper. Cover and simmer over low heat for 1¼ hours, then stir in the coriander and cook for a further 15 minutes, or until the lamb is tender.

MEANWHILE, melt the butter in a frying pan over medium heat, add the almonds and fry them, tossing frequently, for 5 minutes or until golden. Remove immediately to a bowl to prevent them over-browning. Shell and halve the boiled eggs.

ARRANGE the lamb on a serving dish, spoon the sauce over and sprinkle with the almonds (warm the almonds a little first if the butter has congealed). Arrange the eggs on top and scatter with a few coriander leaves.

While these recipes use lamb, in Morocco the sheep is usually over a year old (and would hence be called hogget or mutton in other countries).

LAMB TAGINE WITH QUINCE

THIS SWEET–SOUR DISH OF LAMB WITH QUINCE AND APRICOTS ILLUSTRATES THE EARLY PERSIAN INFLUENCE IN MOROCCAN CUISINE, BUT THE SPICING IS PURE MOROCCAN. IF THE FLAVOUR IS TOO TART FOR YOUR LIKING, ADD SOME HONEY TO TASTE AS WELL AS THE SUGAR.

1.5 kg (3 lb 5 oz) lamb shoulder, cut into 3 cm (1¼ in) pieces
2 large brown onions, diced
½ teaspoon ground ginger
½ teaspoon cayenne pepper
⅛ teaspoon ground saffron threads
1 teaspoon ground coriander
1 cinnamon stick
3 tablespoons roughly chopped coriander (cilantro) leaves
40 g (1½ oz) butter
500 g (1 lb 2 oz) quinces, peeled, cored and quartered
100 g (3½ oz/½ cup) dried apricots
3 tablespoons caster (superfine) sugar
coriander (cilantro) leaves, extra, to serve

SERVES 6–8

PUT the lamb in a heavy-based, flameproof casserole dish and add half the onion, the ginger, cayenne pepper, saffron, ground coriander, cinnamon stick, chopped coriander and some salt and pepper. Add 375 ml (13 fl oz/1½ cups) water and bring to the boil over medium–high heat. Lower the heat and simmer, covered, for 1 hour.

WHILE the lamb is cooking, melt the butter in a heavy-based frying pan and cook the remaining onion and the quinces for 15 minutes over medium heat, or until lightly golden. Add the quince mixture, apricots and sugar to the lamb and cook for 30 minutes, or until the lamb is tender.

TASTE the sauce and adjust the seasoning if necessary. Transfer to a warm serving dish and sprinkle with the extra coriander. Serve with couscous or rice.

While quince discolours when cut, this disappears once cooking begins in the butter–onion mixture.

KSEKSOU TANJAOUI

COUSCOUS WITH LAMB AND RAISINS

THIS IS ONE OF THE SWEET COUSCOUS DISHES SERVED AT DIFFAS (BANQUETS), THE SWEETNESS COMING FROM THE ADDITION OF RICH-TASTING RAISINS. THE LAMB SHANK MEAT COOKS TO MELTING TENDERNESS, BUT OTHER LAMB CUTS CAN BE USED, SUCH AS THICKLY CUT SHOULDER CHOPS.

60 g (2¼ oz) butter
3–5 lamb shanks, depending on
  size, untrimmed
2 brown onions, quartered
½ teaspoon ground turmeric
1½ teaspoons ginger
1 teaspoon freshly ground black
  pepper
⅛ teaspoon ground saffron threads
pinch of cayenne pepper
3 coriander (cilantro) sprigs and
  3 flat-leaf (Italian) parsley sprigs,
  tied in a bunch
420 g (15 oz) tin chickpeas
1 brown onion, extra, halved and
  sliced
90 g (3¼ oz/¾ cup) raisins
1 quantity couscous (page 278)

SERVES 6

HEAT the butter in a large saucepan or the base of a large couscoussier. Add the lamb shanks, onion quarters, turmeric, ginger, black pepper, saffron and cayenne pepper and stir over low heat for 1 minute. Add 500 ml (17 fl oz/ 2 cups) water, the bunch of herbs and 1 teaspoon salt. Bring to a gentle boil, cover and simmer over low heat for 1¾–2 hours, or until the lamb is tender.

MEANWHILE, drain the chickpeas and put them in a large bowl with cold water to cover. Lift up handfuls of chickpeas and rub them between your hands to loosen the skins. Run more water into the bowl, stir well and let the skins float to the top, then skim them off. Repeat until all the skins have been removed. Drain and set aside.

WHEN the lamb is cooked, lift the shanks from the broth and strip off the meat. Discard the bones and cut the meat into pieces. Return the meat to the pan, along with the chickpeas, extra sliced onion and the raisins. Cover and cook for 20 minutes, adding a little more water to the pan if necessary.

WHILE the stew is cooking, prepare the couscous.

PILE the couscous on a large, warm platter and make a dent in the centre. Remove and discard the herbs from the lamb mixture, then ladle it into the hollow. Moisten with some of the broth and put the remaining broth in a bowl, which can be added as needed.

Remove skins from chickpeas so that flavours can penetrate. Trim meat from bones before serving.

Smen has a higher burning point but more flavour than oil. Perfect for browning chicken.

COUSCOUS WITH CHICKEN AND VEGETABLES

THIS IS ONE OF THE MOST FREQUENTLY PREPARED COUSCOUS DISHES IN MOROCCAN HOUSEHOLDS ON FRIDAYS – THE TRADITIONAL DAY FOR SERVING COUSCOUS. THE CHICKEN AND THE VEGETABLES ARE SERVED ON TOP OF THE COUSCOUS AND MOISTENED WITH A HARISSA-FLAVOURED BROTH.

1.6 kg (3 lb 8 oz) chicken
3 tablespoons smen (page 282) or ghee
1 brown onion, finely chopped
½ teaspoon ground turmeric
½ teaspoon ground cumin
8 baby onions, trimmed
¼ teaspoon ground saffron threads
1 cinnamon stick
4 coriander (cilantro) sprigs and 4 flat-leaf (Italian) parsley sprigs, tied in a bunch
3 tomatoes, peeled, seeded and chopped
3 carrots, cut into chunks
4 zucchini (courgettes), cut into chunks
200 g (7 oz/1⅓ cups) shelled green peas, or very young broad (fava) beans
420 g (15 oz) tin chickpeas, rinsed and drained

COUSCOUS
1 quantity couscous (page 278)
3 tablespoons herbed smen (page 282) or butter
3 teaspoons harissa (page 286), or to taste

SERVES 6–8

JOINT the chicken into 8 pieces. You don't need to remove the skin. Heat the smen in a large saucepan or the base of a large couscoussier, add the chicken and brown on each side. Reduce the heat, add the onion and cook until it has softened. Stir in the turmeric and cumin and add the baby onions. Pour in 750 ml (26 fl oz/3 cups) water, then add the saffron, cinnamon stick, the bunch of herbs and the tomato. Season with 1½ teaspoons salt and freshly ground black pepper, to taste. Bring to a gentle boil, cover and cook over low heat for 25 minutes. Add the carrot and simmer for a further 20 minutes. Add the zucchini, green peas and chickpeas and cook for 20 minutes, or until the chicken and vegetables are tender.

WHILE the stew is cooking, prepare the couscous. Stir the herbed smen through the couscous.

SERVE the chicken and vegetables on the couscous. Moisten with some of the broth from the stew. Put 250 ml (9 fl oz/1 cup) of the broth into a bowl and stir in the harissa. The harissa-flavoured broth is added to the couscous to keep it moist, and according to individual taste.

BESTILLA
FESTIVE CHICKEN PIE

TRADITIONALLY THIS FAMOUS MOROCCAN PIE IS MADE WITH PIGEONS, AND THESE ARE GIVEN AS AN ALTERNATIVE. SOLD AS SQUABS, THEY ARE YOUNG PIGEONS SPECIALLY BRED FOR THE TABLE. HOWEVER, CHICKEN IS A POPULAR SUBSTITUTE, EVEN IN MOROCCO.

150 g (5½ oz) smen (page 282) or butter
1.5 kg (3 lb 5 oz) chicken, quartered or 3 x 500 g (1 lb 2 oz) squab pigeons, halved
2 large red onions, finely chopped
3 garlic cloves, crushed
1 cinnamon stick
1 teaspoon ground ginger
1½ teaspoons ground cumin
¼ teaspoon cayenne pepper
½ teaspoon ground turmeric
pinch of saffron threads soaked in 2 tablespoons warm water
500 ml (17 fl oz/2 cups) chicken stock
1 tablespoon lemon juice
3 tablespoons chopped flat-leaf (Italian) parsley
3 tablespoons chopped coriander (cilantro) leaves
5 eggs, lightly beaten
100 g (3½ oz/⅔ cup) blanched almonds, toasted and finely chopped
3 tablespoons icing (confectioners') sugar, plus extra to serve
1 teaspoon ground cinnamon, plus extra to serve
14 sheets filo pastry
100 g (3½ oz) smen (page 282), extra, melted

SERVES 6–8

PREHEAT the oven to 160°C (315°F/Gas 2–3). Melt the smen in a flameproof casserole dish over medium heat and brown the chicken or squab well. Set aside. Add the onion and cook for 10 minutes or until golden. Stir in the garlic and spices, then stir in the saffron, its soaking liquid and the stock. Add chicken and turn to coat. Cover and put in the oven for 1 hour, turning occasionally or until cooked. Add a little extra water if needed. Remove the chicken, reserving the sauce. Discard the cinnamon stick. Remove the meat from the bones and cut into small pieces. Increase the oven temperature to 180°C (350°F/Gas 4).

PUT the reserved sauce, lemon juice and herbs in a saucepan and reduce over high heat for 10 minutes until thick. Reduce the heat to very low, gradually stir in the eggs until scrambled, then remove from the heat. Add the meat and season.

MIX the almonds with the icing sugar and cinnamon. Grease a 30 cm (12 in) pizza pan or pie plate with melted smen. Stack 8 sheets of filo pastry and brush top sheet with smen. Place that sheet evenly across pan with ends overhanging. Repeat with the next 7 sheets, brushing and fanning sheets to cover pan, with pastry overhanging evenly all round. Fill with the chicken mixture and smooth over. Fold four of the flaps back over, brush with smen and sprinkle with the almond mixture. Fold the remaining four sheets over and brush top with smen. Brush remaining six filo sheets with smen, fanning onto pie as before. Using kitchen scissors, cut the overhanging pastry evenly around edge about 3 cm (1¼ in) from edge of pan. Using a rubber spatula to lift edge of pie, tuck overhanging pastry underneath. Bake for 45–50 minutes until golden.

SIFT extra icing sugar over top of pie and make a lattice pattern with extra ground cinnamon.

Assembling the pie using filo pastry. When cooked sift icing sugar over the top. Take pinches of cinnamon between tips of thumb and forefinger and trickle lines in a lattice pattern.

Leave the skin on the apples and turn frequently as they cook in the butter.

TAGINE LHAM BEL TEFFAH WA ZBIB

BEEF TAGINE WITH APPLES AND RAISINS

THIS IS A ROBUST BEEF TAGINE THAT IS SERVED WHEN APPLES ARE IN SEASON, THE TARTNESS OF THE FRUIT MELLOWED WITH THE ADDITION OF RAISINS, SPICES AND HONEY. FOR A REALLY AUTHENTIC FLAVOUR, CHOOSE A THICK, THYME-FLAVOURED HONEY IF POSSIBLE.

1 kg (2 lb 4 oz) beef chuck steak
2 tablespoons olive oil
40 g (1½ oz) butter
1 brown onion, sliced
⅛ teaspoon ground saffron threads
½ teaspoon ground ginger
1 teaspoon ground cinnamon
4 coriander (cilantro) sprigs, tied in a bunch
125 g (4½ oz/1 cup) raisins
3 tablespoons honey
3 tart apples, such as granny smiths
½ teaspoon ground cinnamon, extra
1 tablespoon sesame seeds, toasted

SERVES 6

TRIM the beef and cut into 2.5 cm (1 in) cubes. In a heavy-based saucepan placed over high heat, add half the oil and half the butter and brown the beef in batches. Remove to a dish when browned. Add the remaining oil as needed, and set aside the remaining butter.

REDUCE the heat to medium, add the onion and cook gently for 5 minutes to soften. Sprinkle in the saffron, ginger and cinnamon and cook for 1 minute or so. Add 375 ml (13 fl oz/1½ cups) water, 1½ teaspoons salt and a generous grind of black pepper. Stir well and return the beef to the pan, along with the bunch of coriander sprigs. Cover and simmer over low heat for 1½ hours. Add the raisins and 1 tablespoon of the honey, then cover and simmer for a further 30 minutes, or until the meat is tender.

MEANWHILE, wash the apples, halve and remove the cores. Cut each half into three wedges. Heat the remaining butter in a frying pan and add the apples. Cook for 10 minutes, turning the apples frequently. Drizzle with the remaining honey, dust with the extra cinnamon and cook for 5 minutes, or until glazed and softened.

TRANSFER the meat to a serving dish, pour the sauce over and arrange the apples on top. Serve hot, sprinkled with toasted sesame seeds.

THE COAST

A small pinch of saffron is all that is required to impart the spice's flavour and aroma to these delicious fish balls.

HOUT ZA'FARAN BIL MARAK MATISHA

SAFFRON FISH BALLS IN TOMATO SAUCE

THIS RECIPE WAS DEVISED BY MOROCCAN JEWS, WHO WERE ALSO THE PRINCIPAL GATHERERS OF THE SAFFRON CROCUS WHEN IT WAS INTRODUCED FROM MOORISH SPAIN. IT IS BASED ON THEIR TRADITIONAL RECIPE FOR FISH BALLS, BUT WITH DISTINCTIVE MOROCCAN FLAVOURS.

500 g (1 lb 2 oz) boneless firm white fish fillets
1 egg
2 spring onions (scallions), chopped
1 tablespoon chopped flat-leaf (Italian) parsley
1 tablespoon chopped coriander (cilantro) leaves
55 g (2 oz/⅔ cup) fresh breadcrumbs
small pinch saffron threads

TOMATO SAUCE
500 g (1 lb 2 oz) tomatoes
1 brown onion, coarsely grated
3 tablespoons olive oil
2 garlic cloves, finely chopped
1 teaspoon paprika
½ teaspoon harissa (page 286), or to taste, or ¼ teaspoon cayenne pepper
½ teaspoon ground cumin
1 teaspoon caster (superfine) sugar

SERVES 4

CUT the fish fillets into rough pieces and put in a food processor bowl, along with the egg, spring onion, parsley, coriander and breadcrumbs. Soak the saffron in 1 tablespoon warm water for 5 minutes and add to the other ingredients with ¾ teaspoon salt and some freshly ground black pepper. Process to a thick paste, scraping down the sides of the bowl occasionally.

WITH moistened hands, shape the fish mixture into balls the size of a walnut. Put on a tray, cover and set aside in the refrigerator.

TO MAKE the tomato sauce, first peel the tomatoes by scoring a cross in the base of each one. Put them in a bowl of boiling water for 20 seconds, then plunge into a bowl of cold water to cool. Remove from the water and peel the skin away from the cross – it should slip off easily. Halve the tomatoes crossways and squeeze out the seeds. Chop the tomatoes and set aside.

PUT the onion and olive oil in a saucepan and cook over medium heat for 5 minutes. Add the garlic, paprika, harissa and cumin. Stir for a few seconds, then add the tomato, sugar, 250 ml (9 fl oz/1 cup) water, and salt and freshly ground black pepper, to taste. Bring to the boil, cover, reduce heat and simmer for 15 minutes.

ADD the fish balls to the tomato sauce, shaking the pan occasionally as they are added so that they settle into the sauce. Return to a gentle boil over medium heat, then cover and reduce the heat to low. Simmer for 20 minutes. Serve hot with crusty bread.

HOUT TUNGERA

FISH TAGINE WITH TOMATO AND POTATO

WHEN COOKING FISH IN A TAGINE, MOROCCAN COOKS PREVENT IT FROM STICKING TO THE BASE OF THE TAGINE BY USING CRISSCROSSED BAMBOO CANES, PIECES OF CELERY OR STICKS OF CARROT. POTATO SLICES SERVE THE SAME PURPOSE, AND BECOME A DELICIOUS PART OF THE DISH.

CHERMOULA

2 garlic cloves, roughly chopped
3 tablespoons chopped flat-leaf
    (Italian) parsley
3 tablespoons chopped coriander
    (cilantro) leaves
2 teaspoons paprika
2 teaspoons ground cumin
¼ teaspoon cayenne pepper
1 tablespoon lemon juice
2 tablespoons olive oil

4 x 2 cm (¾ in) thick firm white fish
    steaks, such as snapper or Blue
    Eye
500 g (1 lb 2 oz) potatoes
375 g (13 oz) ripe tomatoes
1 green capsicum (pepper)
1½ tablespoons tomato paste
    (concentrated purée)
1 teaspoon caster (superfine) sugar
1 tablespoon lemon juice
2 tablespoons olive oil
2 tablespoons combined chopped
    flat-leaf (Italian) parsley and
    coriander (cilantro) leaves

SERVES 4

TO MAKE the chermoula, pound the garlic to a paste with ½ teaspoon salt using a mortar and pestle. Add the parsley, coriander, paprika, cumin, cayenne pepper and lemon juice. Pound the mixture to a rough paste and then work in the olive oil.

RUB half the chermoula on each side of the fish, place the fish in a dish, then cover and set aside for 20 minutes.

CUT the potatoes and tomatoes into 5 mm (¼ in) thick slices. Remove the seeds and white membranes from the capsicum and cut into 5 mm (¼ in) thick strips. Preheat the oven to 200°C (400°F/Gas 6).

BRUSH a 30 x 40 x 6 cm (12 x 16 x 2½ in) ovenproof dish with oil. Place a layer of potato slices in the bottom. Put the fish on top. Toss the remaining potato slices with the remaining chermoula and arrange over the fish. Top with the tomato and capsicum strips. Mix the tomato paste with 125 ml (4 fl oz/½ cup) water and add ½ teaspoon salt, a good grinding of black pepper, the sugar, lemon juice and olive oil. Pour over the fish and sprinkle with the mixed herbs.

COVER the dish with foil and bake in the oven for 40 minutes, then remove the foil and move the dish to the upper shelf. Cook for a further 10 minutes, or until the fish and potato are tender and the top is lightly crusted. Serve hot.

Chermoula ingredients being prepared in the time-honoured manner – using a mortar and pounding with a pestle.

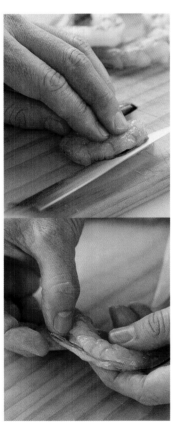

To devein prawns (shrimp), cut a shallow slit along the back to expose the visible vein and pull it out gently.

KEMROON M'HAMMAR

SPICY PRAWNS

M'HAMMAR IS ONE OF THE FOUR BASIC FLAVOURING COMBINATIONS OF MOROCCAN CUISINE, WITH ITS MAIN INGREDIENTS BEING GARLIC, PAPRIKA AND CUMIN. WITH THE ADDITION OF CHOPPED RED CHILLI, THIS PRAWN DISH IS A WORTHY RIVAL TO THE POPULAR GARLIC PRAWNS.

375 g (13 oz) raw prawns (shrimp)
3 tablespoons olive oil
½ teaspoon ground cumin
½ teaspoon cumin seeds
1 teaspoon ground ginger
2 teaspoons chopped red chilli
3 garlic cloves, finely chopped
½ teaspoon ground turmeric
1 teaspoon paprika
2 tablespoons finely chopped
   coriander (cilantro) leaves
lemon wedges, to serve

SERVES 4

PEEL the prawns, leaving the tails intact. To devein the prawns, cut a slit down the back and remove any visible vein. Put the prawns in a colander and rinse under cold running water. Shake the colander to remove any excess water, sprinkle the prawns with ½ teaspoon salt, toss through and set aside.

POUR the olive oil into a large frying pan and place over medium heat. Stir in the ground cumin, cumin seeds, ginger and chilli. Cook until fragrant and the cumin seeds start to pop, then add the garlic, turmeric and paprika. Cook, stirring, for a few seconds, then add the prawns. Increase the heat a little and fry the prawns, tossing frequently, for 3–4 minutes until they firm up and turn pink. Stir in the coriander and 3 tablespoons water, bring to a simmer and remove from the heat. Serve immediately with lemon wedges.

KEMROOM BIL CHERMOULA

PRAWNS WITH HERBS AND PRESERVED LEMON

THERE ARE VARIOUS VERSIONS OF CHERMOULA. IT IS USED WIDELY IN COOKING SEAFOOD, WITH THE PRESERVED LEMON IN THIS VERSION ADDING A DELICATE PIQUANCY. IF YOU DO NOT HAVE PRESERVED LEMON ON HAND, ADD THE ZEST OF HALF A LEMON AND LEMON JUICE TO TASTE.

1 kg (2 lb 4 oz) raw large prawns
  (shrimp)
2 tablespoons olive oil
lemon wedges, to serve
saffron rice (page 281), to serve

CHERMOULA
½ preserved lemon (page 285)
2 garlic cloves, roughly chopped
3 tablespoons chopped flat-leaf
  (Italian) parsley
3 tablespoons chopped coriander
  (cilantro) leaves
⅛ teaspoon ground saffron threads
  (optional)
½ teaspoon paprika
⅛ teaspoon cayenne pepper or
  ½ teaspoon harissa (page 286)
½ teaspoon ground cumin
2 tablespoons lemon juice
3 tablespoons olive oil

SERVES 4

PEEL the prawns, leaving the tails intact. To devein the prawns, cut a slit down the back and remove any visible vein. Place the prawns in a colander and rinse under cold running water. Shake the colander to remove any excess water, sprinkle the prawns with ½ teaspoon salt toss through and set aside.

TO MAKE the chermoula, remove the pulp and membrane from the preserved lemon, rinse the rind and pat dry with paper towel. Chop roughly and place in a food processor bowl, along with the garlic, parsley, coriander, saffron (if using), paprika, cayenne pepper, cumin and lemon juice. Process to a coarse paste, gradually adding the olive oil while processing.

HEAT the olive oil in a large frying pan over medium–high heat, then add the prawns and cook, stirring often, until they begin to turn pink. Reduce the heat to medium, add the chermoula and continue to cook, stirring often, for 3 minutes, or until the prawns are firm. Season to taste. Serve hot with lemon wedges and saffron rice.

In a frying pan, cook the prawns in olive oil, stirring or tossing often, until they stiffen and change colour.

PRAWNS IN CHERMOULA

Spread chermoula on a butterflied sardine, then top with another butterflied sardine and press firmly together. The sandwiched sardines are floured and fried, and served hot.

SARDIN MRAQAD

FRIED SARDINE SANDWICHES

SARDINES ARE AT THEIR BEST WHEN SANDWICHED WITH A FILLING OF CHERMOULA. SOME FISH MERCHANTS SPLIT AND FILLET THEM, CUTTING OFF THE TAILS, BUT IT IS EASY TO DO THIS YOURSELF AND YOU CAN EVEN LEAVE THE TAILS ON FOR EFFECT IF DESIRED.

24 fresh sardines
olive oil, for frying
plain (all-purpose) flour, to dust
lemon wedges, to serve

CHERMOULA STUFFING
1 tablespoon drained grated white
   onion
1 garlic clove, crushed
3 tablespoons finely chopped flat-
   leaf (Italian) parsley
3 tablespoons finely chopped
   coriander (cilantro) leaves
¼ teaspoon cayenne pepper
½ teaspoon paprika
¼ teaspoon freshly ground black
   pepper
½ teaspoon ground cumin
½ teaspoon grated lemon zest
2 teaspoons lemon juice
2 teaspoons olive oil

SERVES 6 AS AN APPETISER

TO BUTTERFLY the sardines, first remove the heads. Cut through the undersides of the sardines and rinse under cold running water. Snip the backbone at the tail with kitchen scissors, without cutting through the skin, and pull carefully away from body starting from the tail end. Open out the sardines and pat the inside surface dry with paper towel. Sprinkle lightly with salt. Set aside.

TO MAKE the stuffing, put the drained onion in a bowl and add the garlic, parsley, coriander, cayenne pepper, paprika, black pepper, cumin, lemon zest and juice, and olive oil. Mix well.

PLACE 12 sardines on a work surface, skin side down. Spread the stuffing evenly on each sardine and cover with another sardine, skin side up. Press them firmly together.

HEAT the olive oil to a depth of 5 mm (¼ in) in a large frying pan. Dust the sardines with flour and fry in the hot oil for 2 minutes on each side, or until crisp and evenly browned. Serve hot with lemon wedges.

HOUT BIL HARISSA WA ZITOUN

FISH WITH HARISSA AND OLIVES

THE SPICY TOMATO SAUCE TAKES ON A BITE WITH THE ADDITION OF HARISSA – ADD WITH CAUTION IF YOU HAVE NOT USED IT BEFORE. AN ALTERNATIVE IS TO ADD ONE TEASPOON OF FINELY CHOPPED RED CHILLI OR A PINCH OF CAYENNE PEPPER. OTHER SUITABLE FISH ARE HAKE AND SEA BASS.

80 ml (2½ fl oz/⅓ cup) olive oil
4 firm white fish fillets, such as Blue Eye, snapper or sea perch
seasoned plain (all-purpose) flour, to dust
1 brown onion, chopped
2 garlic cloves, crushed
400 g (14 oz) tin chopped tomatoes
2 teaspoons harissa (page 286), or to taste
2 bay leaves
1 cinnamon stick
185 g (6½ oz/1 cup) black olives
1 tablespoon lemon juice
2 tablespoons chopped flat-leaf (Italian) parsley

SERVES 4

HEAT half the olive oil in a heavy-based frying pan. Dust the fish fillets with the flour and cook over medium heat for 2 minutes on each side, or until golden. Transfer to a plate.

ADD the remaining olive oil to the pan and cook the onion and garlic for 5 minutes, or until softened. Add the tomatoes, harissa, bay leaves and cinnamon stick. Cook for 10 minutes, or until the sauce has thickened. Season, to taste, with salt and freshly ground black pepper.

RETURN the fish to the pan, add the olives and cover the fish with the sauce. Remove the bay leaves and cinnamon stick and cook for 2 minutes, or until the fish flakes easily with a fork. Add the lemon juice and parsley and serve.

Coat the fish with flour and fry quickly in oil until golden. Complete cooking in the sauce.

CHORBA BIL HOUT

FISH SOUP

WITH SUCH A VARIETY OF FISH AVAILABLE, IT IS SURPRISING THAT THERE ARE SO FEW FISH SOUP RECIPES IN MOROCCAN COOKING. THIS SOUP IS TYPICAL OF THE CUISINE IN TETUAN, IN THE COUNTRY'S NORTH, WHERE SPANISH INFLUENCES STILL PREVAIL.

2 red capsicums (peppers)
1 long red chilli
2 tablespoons extra virgin olive oil
1 brown onion, finely chopped
1 tablespoon tomato paste
   (concentrated purée)
2–3 teaspoons harissa (page 286),
   to taste
4 garlic cloves, finely chopped
2 teaspoons ground cumin
750 ml (26 fl oz/3 cups) fish stock
   (page 281)
400 g (14 oz) tin chopped tomatoes
750 g (1 lb 10 oz) boneless firm
   white fish fillets, cut into
   2 cm (¾ in) cubes
2 bay leaves
2 tablespoons chopped coriander
   (cilantro) leaves

SERVES 6

CUT the capsicums into quarters and remove the membrane and seeds. Cut the chilli in half and remove the seeds. Place the capsicum and chilli pieces, skin side up, under a grill (broiler) and grill (broil) until the skin blackens. Remove and place in a plastic bag, tuck the end of the bag underneath and leave to steam in the bag until cool enough to handle. Remove the blackened skin from the capsicum and the chilli and cut into thin strips. Set aside.

HEAT the oil in a large saucepan and cook the onion for 5 minutes, or until softened. Add the tomato paste, harissa, garlic, cumin and 125 ml (4 fl oz/½ cup) water, then stir to combine. Add the fish stock, tomato and 500 ml (17 fl oz/ 2 cups) water. Bring to the boil, then reduce the heat and add the fish and bay leaves. Simmer for 7–8 minutes, or until the fish is cooked through and opaque.

REMOVE the fish with a slotted spoon and set aside. Discard the bay leaves. When the soup has cooled slightly, add half the chopped coriander and purée in a blender until smooth or use a stick blender in the pan. Season with salt and freshly ground black pepper.

RETURN the soup to the pan if necessary, add the fish, capsicum and chilli and gently reheat. Season to taste. Garnish with the remaining coriander and serve hot with crusty bread.

Remove the blackened skin from grilled chillies. Take out cooked fish before puréeing soup.

A FEAST OF FISH Fishing vessels at Essaouira, ready to be taken out into the Atlantic at 2 am, these days using motor power (top). When the catch arrives mid-morning, customers buy their fish and have it grilled on charcoal fires for a fee. Charcoal fires are fanned, a row of fish-filled wire baskets sizzle, and the fish is served up on plates with lemon wedges (bottom row).

COOKING THE CATCH

MOROCCANS LOVE THEIR FISH. INLAND CITY DWELLERS HEAD FOR THE COAST WHEN THEY WANT THEIR SEAFOOD FRESH, JOINING THE LOCALS FOR THE FEAST. FISH IS AT ITS BEST WHEN COOKED AND EATEN WITHIN SIGHT AND SOUND OF THE SEA, WHILE BREATHING IN THE BRACING SEA AIR.

In places such as Casablanca, Safi and Essaouira, the various catches of the fishermen are inspected, then haggling begins for the best price for their selection. Charcoal grill attendants fan the embers to increase the heat, either using a piece of cardboard in the time-honoured manner, or bowing to modernity with electric fans, their blackened blades evidence of their many months of fanning the embers. Your 'catch' is cooked for a small fee, with an extra fee for grilled tomatoes or eggplant (aubergine) slices. Fish fried in a saffron-coloured batter with fried slices of eggplant and fried chipped potatoes on the side is standard street food, as is a paper bag of freshly fried whitebait. Add to this the picnic tables for eating in comfort and the seaside experience is complete. Fish lovers rejoice!

A sardine vendor sorting the fish according to size (top left). Moroccans catch and process more sardines than anyone else on Earth. A fish vendor proudly showing the prize of the catch – an Atlantic lobster (top right). More sardines in baskets, fresh fish on a slab (bottom left and centre). Chermoula (bottom right), a marinade and/or sauce that marries so well with fish and other seafoods.

CHERMOULA

While fish cooked on the spot might only be anointed with a little oil and sprinkled with salt, the ultimate chargrilled fish would be marinated in chermoula. This marinade and/or sauce is indispensable for cooking fish. It is usually made from a combination of fresh coriander, flat-leaf parsley, garlic, onion, cumin, ground coriander seeds, saffron, paprika and cayenne pepper. Preserved lemon may sometimes be added, or tomatoes, especially the more intensely flavoured semi-dried tomatoes – it all depends on the cook's preference. Chermoula is an excellent basis for cooking prawns and mussels, and is used as a marinade and/or sauce for fish kebabs – keep aside part of the marinade for the sauce; do not use left-over marinade.

LATRWIT BIL TAMRA
TROUT STUFFED WITH DATES

THE MARRIAGE OF DATES WITH FISH IS A TIME-HONOURED PRACTICE IN MOROCCO. TRADITIONALLY THE STUFFED FISH WOULD BE COOKED IN A TAGINE, BUT WITH DOMESTIC OVENS NOW MORE WIDELY AVAILABLE, IT IS OFTEN OVEN-BAKED. THE FOIL WRAPPING KEEPS THE FISH MOIST.

4 medium-sized trout, scaled and cleaned
140 g (5 oz/¾ cup) pitted, chopped dried dates
40 g (1½ oz/¼ cup) cooked rice
4 tablespoons chopped coriander (cilantro) leaves
¼ teaspoon ground ginger
¼ teaspoon ground cinnamon
50 g (1¾ oz/⅓ cup) roughly chopped blanched almonds
1 white onion, finely chopped
40 g (1½ oz) butter, softened
ground cinnamon, to serve (optional)

SERVES 4

PREHEAT the oven to 180°C (350°F/Gas 4). Rinse the trout under cold running water and pat them dry with paper towel. Season lightly with salt and freshly ground black pepper.

COMBINE the dates, cooked rice, coriander, ginger, cinnamon, almonds, half the onion and half the butter in a bowl to make the stuffing. Season well with salt and freshly ground black pepper.

SPOON the stuffing into the fish cavities and place each fish on a well-greased double sheet of foil. Brush the fish with the remaining butter, season with salt and freshly ground black pepper and divide the remaining onion among the four parcels. Wrap the fish neatly and seal the edges of the foil. Place the parcels on a large baking tray and bake for 15–20 minutes, or until flesh is opaque and flakes easily with a fork. If desired, serve dusted with cinnamon.

Spoon the stuffing into the fish cavities before sealing in foil panels to keep moist during cooking.

TUNA SKEWERS WITH HERB MARINADE

TUNA IS IDEAL FOR SKEWERS AS IT IS A FIRM-FLESHED FISH AND DOES NOT FALL APART DURING COOKING. THE CHERMOULA GIVES THE TUNA A FLAVOUR BOOST AND KEEPS IT MOIST. WHILE MOROCCANS COOK TUNA THOROUGHLY, YOU CAN SEAR IT AND SERVE RARE IF DESIRED.

800 g (1 lb 12 oz) tuna steaks, cut into 3 cm (1¼ in) cubes
2 tablespoons olive oil
½ teaspoon ground cumin
2 teaspoons finely grated lemon zest

CHERMOULA
½ teaspoon ground coriander
3 teaspoons ground cumin
2 teaspoons paprika
pinch of cayenne pepper
4 garlic cloves, crushed
3 tablespoons chopped flat-leaf (Italian) parsley
3 tablespoons chopped coriander (cilantro) leaves
80 ml (2½ fl oz/⅓ cup) lemon juice
125 ml (4 fl oz/½ cup) olive oil

SERVES 4

SOAK eight bamboo skewers in water for 2 hours, or use metal skewers.

PUT the tuna in a shallow non-metallic dish. Combine the olive oil, cumin and lemon zest and pour over the tuna. Toss to coat, then cover and marinate in the refrigerator for 10 minutes only.

MEANWHILE, to make the chermoula, put the ground coriander, cumin, paprika and cayenne pepper in a small frying pan and cook over medium heat for 30 seconds, or until fragrant. Combine with the remaining chermoula ingredients and set aside.

THREAD the tuna onto the skewers. Lightly oil a chargrill pan or barbecue grill and cook the skewers for 1 minute on each side for rare, or 2 minutes for medium. Serve with the chermoula drizzled over the tuna.

Thread the marinated fish onto soaked bamboo skewers prior to cooking on a chargrill pan or barbecue grill. In Morocco tuna is cooked through, rather than served rare or medium-cooked.

HOUT BIL HARISSA WAL MATISHA
BAKED FISH WITH HARISSA AND TOMATOES

THE ONIONS PLACED IN THE BASE OF THE ROASTING DISH NOT ONLY ADD FLAVOUR, THEY ALSO PREVENT THE FISH FROM STICKING. THE MOROCCAN METHOD OF EATING WITH ONE'S FINGERS COMES INTO ITS OWN WHEN A WHOLE FISH IS SERVED – IT IS EASY TO FEEL THE BONES!

1 kg (2 lb 4 oz) whole white-fleshed fish, such as snapper or bream, scaled and cleaned
3 garlic cloves, crushed
2 teaspoons harissa (page 286), or to taste
2 tablespoons olive oil
1 lemon, thinly sliced
1 brown onion, thinly sliced
2 large firm, ripe tomatoes, sliced
4 thyme sprigs, plus extra for garnish (optional)

SERVES 4

PREHEAT the oven to 200°C (400°F/Gas 6). Lightly grease a large baking dish. Make three diagonal cuts on each side of the fish through the thickest part of the flesh to ensure even cooking.

COMBINE the garlic, harissa and olive oil in a small dish. Put 2 teaspoons of the harissa mixture in the fish cavity and spread the remainder over both sides of the fish, rubbing it into the slits. Place two lemon slices in the cavity of the fish.

ARRANGE the onion slices in a layer in the baking dish. Top with the tomato slices, thyme and remaining lemon slices. Place the fish on top and bake, uncovered, for about 25–30 minutes, or until the fish flakes at the thickest part, when tested with a fork.

TRANSFER the onion and tomato to a serving dish. Place the fish on top and season with salt. Garnish with extra thyme if desired.

HOUT BENOUA

ALMOND-CRUSTED FISH WITH PRUNES

NORMALLY THIS RECIPE USES WHOLE FISH STUFFED WITH PRUNES, COATED WITH A GROUND-ALMOND MIXTURE AND BAKED. FISH PIECES PAN-FRIED WORKS JUST AS WELL PROVIDING CARE IS TAKEN THAT THE CRUST DOES NOT BURN.

4 x 200 g (7 oz) firm white fish fillets, such as Blue Eye, snapper, hake or sea bass
24 pitted prunes
24 blanched almonds, lightly toasted
30 g (1 oz) butter
2 brown onions, sliced
¾ teaspoon ground ginger
¾ teaspoon ground cinnamon
⅛ teaspoon freshly ground black pepper
⅛ teaspoon ground saffron threads
1½ teaspoons caster (superfine) sugar
3 teaspoons lemon juice
3 teaspoons orange flower water
1 egg
100 g (3½ oz/1 cup) ground almonds
4 tablespoons smen (page 282) or ghee
lemon wedges, to serve

SERVES 4

CHOOSE centre-cut fish fillets no more than 3 cm (1¼ in) thick at the thickest part. Remove the skin (if present) and season lightly with salt. Cover and refrigerate until ready to use. Stuff each prune with a whole toasted almond and set aside.

MELT the butter in a frying pan and add the onion. Cook for 10 minutes over low heat, stirring often, until the onion is soft and golden. Add ½ teaspoon each of the ground ginger and cinnamon, a pinch of salt and the black pepper. Stir for 30 seconds or until fragrant. Pour in 250 ml (9 fl oz/1 cup) water and stir in the saffron. Cover and simmer gently for 5 minutes, then add the stuffed prunes, sugar, lemon juice and orange flower water and stir gently. Cover and simmer for 15 minutes, or until the prunes are plump.

MEANWHILE, beat the egg in a shallow dish with ¼ teaspoon each of ground ginger, cinnamon and salt. Spread the ground almonds in a flat dish. Dip the fish into the beaten egg, drain briefly, and coat on all sides with the ground almonds. Place on a tray lined with baking paper.

MELT the smen in a large non-stick frying pan over medium–high heat (the depth of the smen should be about 5 mm/¼ in). Add the coated fish, reduce the heat to medium and cook for 2 minutes, then turn and cook for a further 2 minutes, or until golden and just cooked through. Do not allow the almond coating to burn. If you have to remove the fish before it is cooked through, place it on top of the onion and prune mixture, cover and simmer gently for 2–3 minutes, taking care that the coating does not become too moist on top. Serve the fish immediately with the onion and prune sauce, with lemon wedges to squeeze over the fish.

The prunes are stuffed with whole almonds for the sauce. Coat the fish with ground almonds.

BESTILLA BEL HOUT

SEAFOOD PIE

THE FAMED BESTILLA CAN ALSO BE MADE WITH A SEAFOOD FILLING, AND MANY RECIPES EXIST. THE EGG YOLKS IN THIS VERSION ARE USED TO THICKEN THE SAUCE, MAKING A MOIST FILLING FULL OF FLAVOURS THAT COMPLEMENT SEAFOODS. GARNISH WITH COOKED PRAWNS IF DESIRED.

3 tablespoons olive oil
1 large white onion, finely chopped
2 garlic cloves, finely chopped
1 teaspoon ground ginger
1 teaspoon ground turmeric
¼ teaspoon cayenne pepper
3 tablespoons chopped flat-leaf
  (Italian) parsley
3 tablespoons chopped coriander
  (cilantro) leaves
½ preserved lemon (page 285),
  chopped
1 kg (2 lb 4 oz) fish fillets, such as
  Blue Eye, sea bass or ling
250 g (9 oz) cooked prawns
  (shrimp), peeled and deveined
375 ml (13 fl oz/1½ cups) fish stock
  (page 281)
pinch of pounded saffron threads
2 tablespoons lemon juice
6 egg yolks
125 g (4½ oz/½ cup) smen
  (page 282) or ghee, melted
11 sheets filo pastry
lemon wedges for serving

SERVES 6

WARM oil in a saucepan, add onion and cook over medium–low heat for 7–8 minutes until very soft. Add garlic, ginger, turmeric and cayenne pepper and stir over heat for 1 minute, then stir in parsley, coriander and preserved lemon. Place fish fillets on top, cover and cook for 10 minutes, until flesh is opaque and flakes easily with a fork. Remove fish to a dish. When cool enough to handle, break into small chunks, removing any skin and bones. Cut the prawns into pieces if large; add to the fish, cover and set aside.

MEANWHILE add the fish stock, saffron and lemon juice to the pan, and boil gently, uncovered, for a further 15 minutes to develop flavours. Whisk egg yolks in a bowl, beat in half the hot liquid from the pan, then return egg mixture to the pan. Stir constantly over low heat until sauce is thick and coats the back of a wooden spoon. Stir in the fish and prawns and season if necessary. Set aside to cool to room temperature.

PREHEAT oven to 180°C (350°F/Gas 4). Grease a 30 cm (12 in) pizza pan with melted smen. Stack 6 sheets filo pastry and brush top sheet with smen. Place evenly across pan with ends overhanging. Repeat with remaining sheets, fanning sheets to cover pan, with pastry overhanging evenly all round. Spread fish filling in pan and fold pastry overhang over filling. Brush with smen. Brush remaining filo sheets with smen, and place on pie, fanning them as before – do not brush last sheet.

USING kitchen scissors, cut pastry evenly around edge about 3 cm (1¼ in) from edge of pan. With a rubber spatula, lift edge of pie, tuck overhang underneath. Brush top with smen and bake for 40 minutes or until golden. Serve with lemon wedges.

The fish is cooked on top of the flavoursome herb–spice mixture. Assembling the seafood pie.

KSEKSOU BEL HOUT

FISH COUSCOUS

IN SEASIDE TOWNS, THE FRIDAY COUSCOUS IS MORE THAN LIKELY TO USE FISH AS THE MAIN INGREDIENT RATHER THAN LAMB OR CHICKEN. THIS IS A SIMPLE COUSCOUS TO MAKE, TYPICALLY HERBED AND SPICED, WITH RICH RED TOMATOES ADDING COLOUR AND FLAVOUR.

750 g (1 lb 10 oz) firm white fish
   fillets, such as snapper, hake or
   sea bass
3 tablespoons plain (all-purpose)
   flour
olive oil
1 large brown onion, finely chopped
2 garlic cloves, finely chopped
½ teaspoon ground cumin
1 teaspoon paprika
¼ teaspoon cayenne pepper
400 g (14 oz) tin chopped tomatoes
125 ml (4 fl oz, ½ cup) fish stock
   (page 281)
1 tablespoon fresh thyme leaves
2 tablespoons chopped flat-leaf
   (Italian) parsley
2 tablespoons chopped coriander
   (cilantro) leaves
pinch of saffron threads
1 quantity couscous (page 278)
60 g (2¼ oz) unsalted butter

SERVES 4–5

CUT fish into 4 cm (1½ in) pieces. In a frying pan, add oil to a depth of 5 mm (¼ in) and place over medium–high heat. Coat fish pieces in flour and fry in the hot oil, turning to brown each side – fish need not be cooked through. Remove to a plate. Discard frying oil.

WIPE pan with paper towel and add 3 tablespoons olive oil and the onion. Cook on medium heat for 5 minutes until soft, add garlic, cumin, paprika and cayenne pepper and cook for a further 1 minute. Add tomatoes, stock, thyme, parsley and coriander. Pound saffron threads with ¼ teaspoon salt, stir into pan contents and season if necessary. Cover and simmer for 20 minutes.

ADD fish, cover and simmer for a further 10 minutes or until fish flakes easily with a fork.

MEANWHILE prepare couscous, add butter to hot couscous and toss with a fork. Serve the fish and sauce over the couscous.

Cut the fish into pieces to flour and fry. Pound saffron threads with a little salt to pulverise.

FISH COUSCOUS

BOUZROUQ

MUSSELS IN TOMATO CHERMOULA SAUCE

IN COASTAL TOWNS AND CITIES, MUSSELS ARE USUALLY ENJOYED IN RESTAURANTS RATHER THAN AT HOME. THE TOMATO CHERMOULA IS A PERFECT SAUCE IN WHICH TO COOK THEM. TAKE CARE IN THE MUSSELS' PREPARATION, AND SERVE WITH PLENTY OF BREAD TO SOAK UP THE DELICIOUS JUICES.

2 kg (4 lb 8 oz) large fresh mussels
3 ripe tomatoes
½ preserved lemon (page 285), chopped
3 tablespoons olive oil
1 large brown onion, finely chopped
2 garlic cloves, finely chopped
1 teaspoon ground cumin
1 teaspoon paprika
⅛ teaspoon cayenne pepper
2 tablespoons chopped flat-leaf (Italian) parsley
2 tablespoons chopped coriander (cilantro) leaves
1 tablespoon lemon juice
coriander (cilantro) leaves, extra, for serving

SERVES 6

SCRUB mussels and beard them if necessary. If any are open, tap them on your bench, and if they don't close, discard. Refrigerate until ready to use.

TO PEEL tomatoes, score a cross in the base of each one. Place tomatoes in a bowl of boiling water and leave for 20 seconds. Drain and cover with cold water. Drain again, and peel the skin away from the cross. Halve tomatoes crossways, and squeeze out the seeds. To prepare preserved lemon, remove the pulp and membranes and rinse the rind under cold water. Chop into small pieces.

IN A large pot, warm the oil, add the onion and cook on medium heat for 5 minutes until soft. Add garlic, cumin, paprika and cayenne pepper. Stir over heat for 1 minute. Add tomatoes, parsley, coriander and preserved lemon. Season, cover and simmer for 15 minutes until tomatoes are soft. Add lemon juice.

ADD prepared mussels, cover pot tightly and cook over high heat until mussels open – about 6–8 minutes – shaking pan occasionally to distribute heat evenly. Divide mussels and sauce into bowls. If any have not opened, return to the pot with a little of the sauce, cover with lid and cook a little longer – if they still have not opened, discard. Sprinkle mussels with coriander leaves and serve hot.

Remove the beards from the mussels when cleaning, then cook in the chermoula sauce.

SWEET DELIGHTS

MULHALABYA
ALMOND CREAM PUDDING

THIS CREAMY MILK PUDDING IS MIDDLE EASTERN IN ORIGIN, THICKENED WITH CORNFLOUR (CORN-STARCH), GROUND RICE AND GROUND ALMOND. ROSEWATER GIVES IT A SUBTLE FRAGRANCE. TOP WITH TOASTED SLIVERED ALMONDS AND A SPRINKLING OF POMEGRANATE SEEDS WHEN IN SEASON.

500 ml (17 fl oz/2 cups) milk
3 tablespoons caster (superfine) sugar
2 tablespoons cornflour (cornstarch)
1 tablespoon ground rice
70 g (2½ oz/⅔ cup) ground almonds
1 teaspoon rosewater
2 tablespoons slivered (or flaked) almonds, toasted
1 teaspoon caster (superfine) sugar, extra
½ teaspoon ground cinnamon

SERVES 4

PUT the milk and sugar in a heavy-based saucepan and heat over medium heat until the sugar has dissolved. Bring to the boil.

MEANWHILE, in a large bowl, combine the cornflour and ground rice with 3 tablespoons water and mix to a smooth paste. Pour in the boiling milk, stirring constantly with a balloon whisk, then return to the saucepan. Stir over medium heat until thickened and bubbling, then add the ground almonds and simmer over low heat for 5 minutes, stirring occasionally until thick and creamy. Add the rosewater and remove from the heat. Stir occasionally to cool a little, then spoon into serving bowls or glasses. Refrigerate for 1 hour.

MIX the toasted almonds with the extra sugar and the cinnamon and sprinkle over the top before serving.

For the best flavour, use freshly blanched almonds. Grind in food processor and add to milk mixture.

ROZZ BIL HLEEB

RICE PUDDING

THIS IS SERVED IN A COMMUNAL DISH IN MOROCCAN HOUSEHOLDS, AND EATEN WITH A SPOON. THE

TOPPING CAN VARY – USUALLY DABS OF BUTTER ARE PLACED ON THE WARM PUDDING, BUT CHOPPED

TOASTED ALMONDS, OR RAISINS AND HONEY AS IN THE RECIPE CAN ALSO BE USED.

110 g (3¾ oz/½ cup) short-grain
   rice
1⅛ litres (39 fl oz/4½ cups) milk
2 tablespoons raisins
2 tablespoons orange flower water
55 g (2 oz/¼ cup) caster (superfine)
   sugar
55 g (2 oz/½ cup) ground almonds
2 tablespoons cornflour (cornstarch)
¼ teaspoon almond extract
2 tablespoons honey

SERVES 8

PUT the rice in a large heavy-based saucepan with 250 ml (9 fl oz/1 cup) water and a pinch of salt. Place over medium heat and cook for 5 minutes, stirring occasionally, until the water has been absorbed.

SET aside 125 ml (4 fl oz/½ cup) of the milk. Stir 250 ml (9 fl oz/1 cup) of the remaining milk into the rice, bring to a simmer, and when the rice has absorbed the milk, add another 250 ml (9 fl oz/ 1 cup) milk. Continue to add the remaining milk in this manner, ensuring each addition of milk is absorbed before adding the next, which will prevent the milk from boiling over. The rice should be very soft in 30 minutes, with the final addition of milk barely absorbed.

MEANWHILE, steep the raisins in 2 teaspoons of the orange flower water for 15 minutes.

MIX the sugar with the ground almonds to break up any lumps in the almonds. Stir into the rice mixture and simmer gently for 2–3 minutes. Mix the cornflour with the reserved milk until smooth and stir into the rice. When thickened, simmer for 2 minutes. Remove the pan from the heat and stir in the almond extract and the remaining orange flower water. Stir the pudding occasionally to cool it a little.

POUR the pudding into a serving bowl and when a slight skin forms on the top, sprinkle with the soaked raisins and drizzle with honey. Cool completely before serving in individual bowls.

As ready-prepared ground almonds can be lumpy, mix with the sugar to break up lumps.

KERMOUS HELWA

FIGS IN SYRUP

DRIED FIGS ARE A POPULAR SNACK FOOD AS THEY ARE, BUT IN WINTER THEY ARE SOAKED AND COOKED WITH TYPICAL MOROCCAN SPICES, TURNING THEM INTO A FRUIT COMPOTE. WHILE NOT TRADITIONAL, YOGHURT CAN BE SERVED WITH THEM.

375 g (13 oz) dried figs
blanched almonds, one per fig
3 whole cloves
3 bruised cardamom pods
½ teaspoon black peppercorns
115 g (4 oz/½ cup) caster (superfine) sugar
thinly peeled zest of ½ lemon
1 cinnamon stick
yoghurt, to serve

SERVES 4–6

RINSE figs under cold, running water and place in a bowl with fresh water to cover generously. Soak for 8 hours until plump. Drain the soaking water into a saucepan. Insert a blanched almond into each fig from the base. Tie spices in a piece of muslin (cheesecloth). Stir sugar into the soaking liquid in saucepan, over medium–high heat, until sugar dissolves. Bring to the boil, add the bag of spices, lemon zest, cinnamon stick and figs. Return to the boil, then reduce to a simmer, and cook, uncovered, for 30 minutes until tender. Transfer figs to a serving dish with a slotted spoon and strain syrup over them. Serve warm or chilled with thick yoghurt.

SFARGEL HELWA BIL MA'EL WARD

QUINCES IN ROSEWATER SYRUP

QUINCES REQUIRE LENGTHY COOKING TO TAKE ON AN ATTRACTIVE ROSY HUE. LEAVING THE SKIN AND CORE ON SHORTENS THE PROCESS; IT IS EASY TO PULL OFF THE SKIN ONCE COOKED. ROSEWATER IS A GOOD FLAVOURING FOR QUINCES, ITS FLORAL TONES ENHANCING THEIR FLAVOUR.

2 quinces, washed well and quartered
175 g (6 oz/¾ cup) caster (superfine) sugar
thinly peeled zest of ½ lemon
2–3 teaspoons rosewater

SERVES 4–6

PLACE quince in a saucepan and cover with water. Bring to the boil, cover and simmer on low heat for 40 minutes until almost tender and beginning to colour. Drain in a fine sieve over a bowl and return liquid to saucepan.

ADD sugar and lemon zest to the pan and stir over heat until sugar dissolves then leave to simmer gently without stirring while you prepare the quince. Pull skin from quince quarters, remove cores and halve each quarter. Place quince slices in the syrup with rosewater to taste and simmer, uncovered, for a further 30 minutes until tender and quinces have a rosy hue. Remove lemon zest and serve warm or chilled.

QUINCES IN ROSEWATER
SYRUP

KERMOUS MA'EL WARD B'LOUZ WA 'ASSEL

FIGS WITH ROSEWATER, ALMONDS AND HONEY

FRESH FIGS ARE ONE OF THE DELIGHTS OF LATE SUMMER AND AUTUMN. WHILE PERFECT ON THEIR OWN, THEY ARE SOMETIMES PREPARED IN THIS WAY AND LOOK VERY ATTRACTIVE SERVED AT THE END OF A BANQUET, WITH THEIR PINK FLOWER INTERIOR EXPOSED.

12 fresh purple-skinned figs
50 g (1¾ oz/⅓ cup) blanched
   almonds, lightly toasted
3–4 teaspoons rosewater
1–2 tablespoons honey

SERVES 6

WASH the figs gently and pat them dry with paper towel. Starting from the stem end, cut each fig into quarters, almost to the base, then gently open out and put on a serving platter. Cover and chill in the refrigerator for 1 hour, or until needed.

ROUGHLY chop the toasted almonds and set aside.

CAREFULLY drizzle about ¼ teaspoon of the rosewater onto the exposed centres of each of the figs, and sprinkle the chopped almonds over the top. Drizzle a little honey over the nuts. Serve immediately.

DALAAH BIL MA'EL WARD WAL NA'NA'

WATERMELON WITH ROSEWATER AND MINT

IN SUMMER, CHILLED WATERMELON IS A GREAT WAY TO FINISH A MEAL. FOR A SPECIAL MEAL OR BANQUET, IT IS OFTEN PRESENTED CUBED AND SEEDED FOR EASE OF EATING. ROSEWATER AND MINT COMPLEMENT THE CRISP, SWEET MELON WITH THEIR FRESH AND FLORAL TONES.

2 kg (4 lb 8 oz) wedge of
   watermelon
3 teaspoons rosewater
small, fresh mint leaves, to serve

SERVES 4–6

WORKING over a plate to catch any juice, remove the skin and the rind from the watermelon and cut the flesh into 2.5 cm (1 in) cubes, removing any visible seeds. Pile the cubes in a bowl. Pour the watermelon juice into a small jug and stir in rosewater. Sprinkle over the watermelon, cover and chill in refrigerator for 1 hour or until required. Scatter with small fresh mint leaves and serve chilled.

WATERMELON WITH
ROSEWATER AND MINT

FIGS WITH ROSEWATER, ALMONDS AND HONEY

PICK YOUR PASTRY An Aladdin's 'cave' of Moroccan multi-hued cookies and pastries (left), awaiting shoppers who will buy a treat to have with their mint tea. They include cookies, pastries and sweet rusks, French-style 'boats' ready to be filled with patisserie cream (top centre), almond filo coils (top right), or one of the Moroccan and French pastries (below centre) next to *briouat* (below right).

PASTRY SHOP

THE POPULARITY OF MOROCCAN AND FRENCH PASTRIES IS CONFIRMED WITH THE NUMBER OF PASTRY SHOPS, OPEN-FRONTED, DECORATIVE STALLS, OR MERELY A VENDOR GUARDING HIS GLASS CABINET STACKED WITH HIS SPECIALTIES. ONE CONSTANT IS THAT YOU ARE SELDOM DISAPPOINTED WITH YOUR CHOICES.

Moroccan pastries have links to those of the Middle East, but are completely different in their final form. *Ghoriba* are found from the Middle East to Morocco in various forms, but Moroccans make *baklawa*-type pastries their way – unique and just as delicious. The similarities are in the ingredients used – almonds, cinnamon, orange flower water, rosewater, a hint of lemon zest, honey – these are the popular ingredients for making many of these sweet delicacies. Walnuts, dates, raisins, dried figs, caraway and sesame seeds are also used according to the art of the pâtissière.

While filo pastry is used in recipes, *warkha* is the only pastry used in Morocco. Its pedigree is Persian, and it was perfected in palace kitchens. Delicate and tissue thin, it is

Warkha pastry sheets are carefully separated by a pâtissière for making various sweet pastries (left) – *briouat* with various fillings, shaped in triangles, rolls or coils to be fried and dipped in syrup or baked to perfection. Shelves of various French and Moroccan sweet delights – meringues and other French patisserie with Moroccan sweet rusks and Gazelles' Horns both plain and coated (right).

made by a process that is now left to experts. A sticky, unleavened dough is prepared, rested and divided into small balls. The *warkha* maker inverts a *tobsil*, a round, tinned copper pan, over a charcoal brazier in which the heat has been carefully controlled with ash. When heated, the *tobsil* is rubbed with an oily cloth. A ball of dough is rapidly tapped repeatedly onto the heated *tobsil*. This continues in a rhythmic way until the dabs of dough join to form a complete sheet. When it is dry around the edges, each sheet is peeled off and placed in a stack. The process is so rapid that a sheet is usually made in a matter of seconds. The first two or three often fail, but after that, perfect sheets are peeled off every time, provided that the *tobsil* is oiled between making each sheet.

KENEFFA

CRISP PASTRIES WITH ALMOND CREAM

FRIED WARKHA PASTRY IS USED FOR THIS TRADITIONAL DESSERT ASSEMBLED IN A TALL STACK WITH ALMOND CREAM AND ALMONDS. IT COLLAPSES WHEN PORTIONS ARE BROKEN OFF WITH THE FINGERS BUT MAKING INDIVIDUAL PASTRY STACKS WITH WON TON WRAPPERS SOLVES THIS PROBLEM.

ALMOND CREAM
750 ml (26 fl oz/3 cups) milk
35 g (1¼ oz/¼ cup) cornflour
   (cornstarch)
60 g (2¼ oz/¼ cup) caster
   (superfine) sugar
50 g (1¾ oz/½ cup) ground
   almonds
¼ teaspoon almond extract
1½ tablespoons rosewater
100 g (3½ oz/⅔ cup) blanched
   almonds, lightly toasted
2 tablespoons icing (confectioners')
   sugar, sifted, plus extra, to serve
½ teaspoon ground cinnamon
36 square won ton wrappers,
   brought to room temperature
vegetable oil, for frying
unsprayed rose petals, to serve

SERVES 6

TO MAKE the almond cream, put 125 ml (4 fl oz/ ½ cup) of the milk in a large bowl, add the cornflour and mix to a thin paste. Bring the remaining milk to the boil until it froths up. Mix the cornflour paste again, then pour in the boiling milk, mixing constantly with a balloon whisk. Pour this back into the saucepan and stir in the sugar and ground almonds. Return to the heat; stir constantly with a wooden spoon until thickened and bubbling. Pour back into the bowl and stir in the almond extract and rosewater. Press a piece of plastic wrap on the surface and leave to cool. Just before using the cream, stir briskly with a balloon whisk to smooth it; if it is too thick, stir in a little milk to give a pouring consistency.

ROUGHLY chop the toasted almonds, mix with the icing sugar and cinnamon, and set aside. Lightly brush a won ton wrapper with water and press another firmly on top. Repeat until there are 18 pairs.

IN A large, deep frying pan, add oil to a depth of 1 cm (½ in) and place over high heat. When the oil is hot, but not smoking, reduce the heat to medium and add two pairs of won ton wrappers. Fry for about 20 seconds until lightly browned, turning to brown evenly. Remove pastries with tongs and drain on paper towel. Repeat with the remaining squares.

TO ASSEMBLE the pastries, put a fried pastry square in the centre of each plate. Drizzle with a little almond cream and sprinkle with a heaped teaspoon of the chopped almond mixture. Repeat with another pastry square, cream and almonds. Finish with another pastry square. Scatter with unsprayed rose petals, sift a little icing sugar over the top and serve with the remaining almond cream in a pitcher.

Brush a won ton wrapper lightly with water and press another firmly on top. Fry in hot oil.

SEFFA

SWEET COUSCOUS

COUSCOUS IS SERVED AS THE FINAL SAVOURY DISH OF A BANQUET AND INTERESTINGLY A SWEET COUSCOUS IS OFTEN SERVED. AS IT IS A POPULAR DISH AT PALACE BANQUETS, THE MORE EXPENSIVE NUTS – PISTACHIOS AND PINE NUTS – ARE OFTEN USED ALONG WITH THE TRADITIONAL ALMONDS.

80 g (2¾ oz, ½ cup) combined pistachio nuts, pine nuts and blanched almonds
40 g (1½ oz/¼ cup) dried apricots
250 g (9 oz/1⅓ cups) instant couscous
55 g (2 oz/¼ cup) caster (superfine) sugar
90 g (3¼ oz) unsalted butter, softened
2 tablespoons caster (superfine) sugar, extra
½ teaspoon ground cinnamon
375 ml (13 fl oz/1½ cups) hot milk

SERVES 4–6

PREHEAT the oven to 160°C (315°F/Gas 2–3). Spread the nuts on a baking tray and bake for about 5 minutes, or until lightly golden. Allow to cool, then roughly chop and place in a bowl. Slice the apricots into matchstick-sized pieces. Add to the bowl with the nuts and toss to combine.

PUT the couscous and sugar in a large bowl and cover with 250 ml (9 fl oz/1 cup) boiling water. Stir well, then add the butter and a pinch of salt. Stir until the butter melts. Cover with a tea towel (dish towel) and set aside for 10 minutes. Fluff the grains with a fork, then toss through half the fruit and nut mixture.

TO SERVE, pile the warm couscous in the centre of a platter. Arrange the remaining nut mixture around the edge. Combine the extra sugar and the cinnamon in a small bowl and serve separately for sprinkling. Pass around the hot milk in a pitcher for guests to help themselves.

AMALOU

ALMOND AND HONEY SPREAD

100 g (3½ oz/1 cup) ground almonds
2 tablespoons argan, walnut or macadamia nut oil
1 tablespoon dark honey
3–4 drops almond extract

MAKES 140 G (5 OZ/½ CUP)

IN A bowl, mix ground almonds with a pinch of salt and nut oil. Stir well and mix in honey and almond extract. The amalou should have a soft, spreading consistency; if necessary mix in a little more oil and honey. The amount of oil depends on the moistness of the ground almonds. Serve spread on bread, *beghrir* (semolina pancakes, page 59) or other pancakes with additional honey if desired. The amalou can be stored in a sealed jar in the refrigerator for 3–4 weeks; bring to room temperature for serving.

ALMOND AND HONEY SPREAD

It is important to work quickly when making each roll to avoid the coils breaking.

M'HANNCHA

ALMOND FILO COIL

M'HANNCHA, MEANING 'SNAKE', IS AN ALMOND PASTE-FILLED PASTRY MADE WITH MOROCCO'S WARKHA PASTRY (FILO PASTRY IS A GOOD SUBSTITUTE). THE PASTRY IS SERVED AT CELEBRATIONS, WITH GUESTS BREAKING OFF PIECES FROM THE COIL. SERVE WITH MINT TEA OR COFFEE.

1 small egg, separated
200 g (7 oz/2 cups) ground
    almonds
30 g (1 oz/⅓ cup) flaked almonds
125 g (4½ oz/1 cup) icing
    (confectioners') sugar
1 teaspoon finely grated lemon zest
¼ teaspoon almond extract
1 tablespoon rosewater
90 g (3¼ oz) unsalted butter or
    smen (page 282), melted
9 sheets filo pastry
pinch of ground cinnamon
icing (confectioners') sugar, extra, to
    serve

SERVES 8

PREHEAT the oven to 180°C (350°F/Gas 4). Lightly grease a 20 cm (8 in) round spring-form tin.

PUT the egg white in a bowl and beat lightly with a fork. Add the ground almonds and flaked almonds, the icing sugar, lemon zest, almond extract and rosewater. Mix to a paste.

DIVIDE the mixture into four and roll each portion on a cutting board into a sausage shape about 5 cm (2 in) shorter than the length of filo pastry – about 42 cm (16½ in) long and 1 cm (½ in) thick. If the paste is too sticky to roll, dust the cutting board with icing sugar.

KEEP the melted butter warm by placing the saucepan in another pan filled with hot water. Remove one sheet of filo pastry and place the rest in the folds of a dry tea towel (dish towel) or cover them with plastic wrap to prevent them from drying out. Brush the filo sheet with the butter, then cover with another sheet of filo, brushing the top with butter. Ease one almond 'sausage' off the board onto the buttered pastry, laying it along the length of the pastry, 2½ cm (1 in) in from the base and sides. Roll up to enclose the filling. Form into a coil and sit the coil, seam side down, in the centre of the tin, tucking under the unfilled ends of the pastry to enclose the filling. Continue in this manner to make three more pastry 'snakes', shaping each around the smaller coil to make a large coil. If the coil breaks, cut small pieces of the remaining filo sheet, brush with a little egg yolk and press the filo onto the breaks.

ADD the cinnamon to the remaining egg yolk and brush over the coil. Bake for 30–35 minutes, or until golden brown. Dust with the extra icing sugar if desired and serve warm. This sweet pastry can be stored at room temperature for up to 2 days.

'ASSEL DDWAZ DATAY

FRIED HONEY CAKES

WHILE YEAST DOUGHS ARE USUALLY PREPARED FOR SWEETS SUCH AS THESE DELICIOUS HONEY CAKES, HERE EGGS AND BAKING POWDER ARE USED TO GIVE THE DESIRED LIGHTNESS WITHOUT THE NEED FOR LENGTHY KNEADING OF THE DOUGH.

3 eggs
3 tablespoons orange juice
3 tablespoons vegetable oil
1 tablespoon grated orange zest
60 g (2¼ oz/¼ cup) caster
   (superfine) sugar
300 g (10½ oz/2½ cups) plain
   (all-purpose) flour
1 teaspoon baking powder
about 4 tablespoons plain
   (all-purpose) flour, extra
vegetable oil, for deep-frying

SYRUP
2 tablespoons lemon juice
275 g (9¾ oz/1¼ cups) caster
   (superfine) sugar
115 g (4 oz/⅓ cup) honey
1 tablespoon grated orange zest

SERVES 4–6

WHISK the eggs, orange juice and oil together in a large bowl. Add the orange zest and sugar and whisk until frothy. Sift in the flour and baking powder and mix with a wooden spoon until smooth, but still a little sticky.

TO MAKE the syrup, put 310 ml (10¾ fl oz/ 1¼ cups) cold water, the lemon juice and sugar in a saucepan and heat, stirring until the sugar dissolves. Bring to the boil, reduce the heat and simmer for 5 minutes. Add the honey and orange zest and then simmer for another 5 minutes. Keep warm.

SPRINKLE a little of the extra flour onto the dough and transfer it to a lightly floured surface. Work in just enough extra flour to give a dough that doesn't stick to your hands. Roll out to a thickness of 5 mm (¼ in). It will be very elastic, so keep rolling and resting it until it stops shrinking. Using a 5 cm (2 in) biscuit cutter, cut out round cakes.

HEAT the oil in a large deep-sided frying pan to 170°C (325°F), or until a cube of bread dropped into the oil browns in 20 seconds. Fry the cakes three or four at a time until puffed and golden – about 1 minute on each side. Remove with tongs and drain on paper towel.

USING tongs, dip each cake into the warm honey syrup, long enough for it to soak in. Transfer to a platter. Serve warm or cold.

Fry honey cakes in hot oil, only 3–4 at a time, so that the oil remains hot. If fried too slowly, the cakes absorb too much oil.

DATE AND NUT CANDIES

THE BERBERS, ESPECIALLY NOMADIC TRIBES, DEPENDED HEAVILY ON THE DATE AS A FOOD. THEY WOULD MAKE DATES INTO SWEETMEATS WITH A RANGE OF OTHER INGREDIENTS. THE INCLUSION OF SMEN AND NUTS INCREASES THE ENERGY VALUE OF THIS PARTICULAR SWEETMEAT.

150 g (5½ oz/1½ cups) walnut halves or 155 g (5¾ oz/1 cup) blanched almonds
2 tablespoons sesame seeds
100 g (3½ oz) smen (page 282), or ghee
600 g (1 lb 5 oz/3⅓ cups) pitted dried dates, roughly chopped

SERVES 6–8

PREHEAT the oven to 180°C (350°F/Gas 4) and line the base of an 18 cm (7 in) square baking tin with baking paper. Ensure the paper overhangs the opposite ends of the tin – this will assist you in removing the mixture from the tin later on. Spread the nuts on a baking tray and bake for 5 minutes, or until lightly toasted. Chop roughly. Bake the sesame seeds on a tray for a few minutes or until golden.

MELT the smen in a large heavy-based saucepan. Add the dates and cook, covered, over low heat for about 10 minutes, stirring often, until the dates soften. Remove from heat. Using the back of a spoon dipped in cold water, spread half the dates over the base of the prepared tin. Scatter the nuts on top and press into the dates. Spread the remaining date mixture over the nuts. Smooth the surface with wet fingers and press down firmly.

SPRINKLE with the sesame seeds and press lightly into the dates. Set aside and when cool, remove the set mixture from the tin using the overhanging baking paper as handles. Remove the paper and cut into small diamonds to serve.

This date sweetmeat is both flavoursome and healthy – so easy to make too.

THE ARGAN TREE The fruit (drupes) of the argan tree (top left) which contain the seed. Bottles of reddish-coloured argan oil on sale (below left). An argan tree with goats feeding on the fruit (right). Years ago it was noticed that the goats could not digest the nuts; these were gathered by villagers and once the nut was cracked, the kernel proved to be edible and delicious.

ARGAN OIL

OUTSIDE MOROCCO LITTLE IS KNOWN ABOUT ARGAN OIL, LET ALONE THE ARGAN TREE. HOWEVER, THAT IS CHANGING AS IT HAS BEEN FOUND THAT THE OIL FROM THE DELICIOUS NUT HAS AMAZING PROPERTIES. NOT ONLY HAS IT GREAT POTENTIAL IN COSMETICS, IT HAS BEEN FOUND TO LOWER BAD CHOLESTEROL AND INCREASE THE GOOD.

The argan tree only grows in one area in the world – inland from the Atlantic coast in south-west Morocco, between the cities of Essaouira and Agadir. There are 21 million argan trees in the region, and word has reached the outside world that this gnarled, twisted, scraggy tree is another miracle of nature with great potential.

Village women would crack the nuts between two stones, removing the skin to reveal two or three oval, blanched almond-like nuts. Besides being a tasty treat, it was found that by roasting them lightly, pounding or grinding, then kneading the resultant paste, the oil that separated out was a very tasty oil indeed. It was used for cooking, added to couscous, and used as a cosmetic and a cure for acne.

Women working on the nuts, sorting, separating nuts from cracked shells, removing the skins from the nuts (top left). Cracking the nuts on a stone with a smaller stone (below left and top right). The nuts in their skins, removed as you would when blanching almonds (below centre). The cleaned nuts (below right) ready for bagging before further processing.

A string of cottage industries has evolved, and now there are Women's Cooperatives that are improving production without women losing much-needed income.

The women no longer have the onerous task of grinding the nuts and kneading the paste, although they have old-fashioned earthenware grinders to demonstrate this stage to tourists. Today the cooperatives gather the fruit and strip off the soft outer layer. Bags of nuts are allocated to each group of women, who return the cleaned nuts. These are roasted and ground at each cooperative's plant. It takes 62 kg of nuts to produce 1 litre of argan oil; when the women undertook the whole process, 20 hours of work were required to extract 1 litre of argan oil.

253

BRIOUAT BIL FAKIYA

DRIED FRUIT PASTRIES

FOR THESE PASTRIES, USE THE SOFTER DESSERT FIGS IF POSSIBLE. THE PASTRIES WILL KEEP IN A SEALED CONTAINER FOR 2–3 DAYS IF NECESSARY. IF THE WEATHER IS HUMID, WAIT UNTIL JUST BEFORE SERVING TO SIFT THE ICING SUGAR ON TOP.

125 g (4½ oz) smen (page 282), melted
165 g (5¾ oz/1 cup) blanched almonds
80 g (2¾ oz/½ cup) pitted, chopped dates
80 g (2¾ oz/½ cup) chopped dessert figs (soft, dried figs)
1 tablespoon orange flower water
12 sheets filo pastry
icing (confectioners') sugar, to serve

MAKES 18

IN A small frying pan, warm 1 tablespoon of the smen, add the almonds and cook over medium heat, stirring often, until golden. Tip immediately into the food processor bowl, along with any smen from the pan. Cool, then process until the almonds are finely chopped. Add the dates, figs and orange flower water and process to a thick paste, scraping down the side of the bowl as necessary. Turn out onto the work surface, rub your hands with a little of the smen and gather the paste into a ball. Roll into a sausage 23 cm (9 in) long and cut into 18 equal pieces. Roll each piece into a 10 cm (4 in) log and set aside on baking paper.

COUNT out 12 sheets of filo pastry. Stack these on a cutting surface with the longer side in front of you. Measure and mark pastry in three equal strips and cut through the stack with a sharp knife to create strips 12½–14 cm (4½–5½ in) wide and 28–30 cm (11¼–12 in) long. Stack the strips in the folds of a dry tea towel (dish towel). (Use extra sheets if filo is less than 38 cm (15 in) long.)

PLACE a strip of pastry with the narrow end nearest you and brush with the warm, melted smen. Top with another strip and brush top with smen. Place shaped filling 1½ cm (⅝ in) in from base and sides of strip. Fold end of filo over filling, fold in sides and brush side folds with smen. Roll to the end and place seam side down on a greased baking tray. Repeat with remaining ingredients. Preheat oven to 180°C (350°F/Gas 4) after rolls are completed to keep kitchen cool while shaping.

BRUSH tops of rolls lightly with smen and bake for 20 minutes until lightly golden. Sift icing sugar over rolls while hot. Store when cool in a sealed container. Use within 3 days.

When working with filo, keep the kitchen cool, then preheat the oven.

Brush half the width of the filo strip with butter, then fold in half and butter top. Fold end of strip over filling to line up with side, then straight up and to the other side until end of strip is reached.

HONEY-DIPPED BRIOUATS WITH ALMOND PASTE

THESE CRISP, HONEY-DIPPED PASTRIES ARE FILLED WITH A DELICIOUS ALMOND PASTE FRAGRANT WITH ORANGE FLOWER WATER. WHEN BOILING HONEY FOR DIPPING, IT IS IMPORTANT TO ADD WATER OTHERWISE THE HONEY BURNS.

ALMOND FILLING
200 g (7 oz/2 cups) ground
   almonds
60 g (2 oz) unsalted butter
60 g (2¼ oz/½ cup) icing
   (confectioners') sugar
¼ teaspoon almond extract
1 tablespoon orange flower water

PASTRY WRAPPING
6 sheets filo pastry
125 g (4½ oz) smen (page 282),
   melted

HONEY SYRUP
260 g (9¼ oz/¾ cup) honey
1 tablespoon orange flower water

MAKES 18

PLACE a heavy-based saucepan on medium heat, add ground almonds and stir constantly until lightly toasted – about 3–4 minutes. Quickly tip into a bowl, add the butter and stir until it melts. When cool, add remaining almond filling ingredients and mix thoroughly to a paste.

STACK the filo sheets on a cutting board with the longer side in front of you and, with a ruler and sharp knife, measure and cut into strips 12–14 cm (4½–5½ in) wide and 28–30 cm (11¼–12 in) long. Stack the strips and cover with a dry, folded cloth to prevent them from drying out.

PLACE a filo strip on a work surface, brush half the width with smen and fold in half to give a strip about 6 cm (2½ in) wide. Brush over the top with smen and place a heaped teaspoon of the almond filling towards the end of the strip. Fold end diagonally across filling so that base lines up with side of strip, forming a triangle. Fold straight up once, then fold diagonally to opposite side; continue to end of strip, trimming excess pastry with scissors. Place, seam side down, on a lightly greased baking tray. Repeat with remaining ingredients and brush tops lightly with smen.

PREHEAT the oven to 180°C (350°F/Gas 4); do this after triangles are completed, so that the kitchen remains cool while shaping. Bake pastries for 20–25 minutes or until puffed and golden.

TOWARDS end of cooking, combine honey syrup ingredients with ¼ cup (60 ml/2 fl oz) water in a 1.5 litre (52 fl oz/6 cup) saucepan. Bring to the boil and reduce heat to low. Dip hot pastries, two at a time, in the syrup, leave for 20 seconds and remove with two forks to a tray lined with baking paper. As pastries are dipped, honey boils up in pan, so take care. Cool and serve on the day of baking.

GHORIBA B'LOOZ

ALMOND MACAROONS

THESE ALMOND BISCUITS ARE DIPPED INTO POWDERED SUGAR BEFORE BAKING. DURING BAKING, THEY RISE A LITTLE AND THE SUGAR TOPPING BECOMES CRACKLED. MOROCCAN COOKS BAKE THESE BISCUITS IN A COMMUNAL OVEN, TO BE ENJOYED LATER WITH MINT TEA.

300 g (10½ oz/3 cups) ground
   almonds
150 g (5½ oz/1¼ cups) icing
   (confectioners') sugar
1½ teaspoons baking powder
½ teaspoon ground cinnamon
1 egg
2 teaspoons grated lemon zest
1 tablespoon rosewater
3 tablespoons icing (confectioners')
   sugar, extra

MAKES ABOUT 36

PUT the ground almonds in a mixing bowl and sift in the icing sugar, baking powder and cinnamon. Stir well to mix the dry ingredients thoroughly. Beat the egg with the lemon zest and rosewater and add to the dry ingredients. Mix to a firm paste and knead lightly.

LINE two baking trays with baking paper. Sift the extra icing sugar into a shallow dish. Preheat the oven to 180°C (350°F/Gas 4).

BREAK off pieces of dough the size of walnuts and roll them into balls, oiling your hands lightly to prevent the dough sticking. Press the balls into the extra sifted icing sugar and flatten slightly. Lift carefully so that the topping is not disturbed, and place on the baking trays, sugar side up, spacing them 5 cm (2 in) apart to allow for spreading. Bake for 20 minutes. Leave the macaroons on the trays for 10 minutes before removing to a wire rack to cool. Store in an airtight container.

Flattened balls of dough are dipped in icing sugar and placed sugar side up for baking.

SESAME COOKIES

SESAME SEEDS STAR IN THESE DELICIOUS BISCUITS. THEIR NUTTY FLAVOUR IS ACCENTUATED WHEN
ROASTED, BUT TAKE CARE THAT THE SEEDS DO NOT BURN. THEY CAN BE BOUGHT FROM PATISSERIES
IN THE CITIES, TO BE TAKEN HOME OR TO A NEARBY CAFÉ TO ENJOY WITH MINT TEA OR COFFEE.

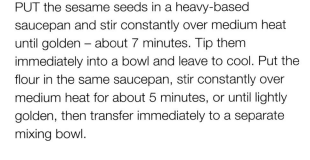

225 g (8 oz/1½ cups) sesame
    seeds
150 g (5½ oz/1¼ cups) plain
    (all-purpose) flour, sifted
165 g (5¾ oz/¾ cup) caster
    (superfine) sugar
1½ teaspoons baking powder
2 eggs, beaten
1 tablespoon orange flower water
2–3 tablespoons sesame seeds,
    extra

MAKES ABOUT 36

PUT the sesame seeds in a heavy-based
saucepan and stir constantly over medium heat
until golden – about 7 minutes. Tip them
immediately into a bowl and leave to cool. Put the
flour in the same saucepan, stir constantly over
medium heat for about 5 minutes, or until lightly
golden, then transfer immediately to a separate
mixing bowl.

WHEN the sesame seeds are cool, put them in a
blender and process until reduced almost to a
powder (this is best done in two batches as it is
difficult to process the seeds efficiently in one
batch). Some seeds should remain visible after
processing. Add to the flour, along with the caster
sugar and baking powder and mix thoroughly.
Make a well in the centre and add the beaten eggs
and orange flower water. Stir into the dry
ingredients, then knead well until smooth.

PUT the extra sesame seeds in a shallow dish.
Line two baking trays with baking paper or grease
them well with butter. Preheat the oven to 180°C
(350°F/Gas 4).

BREAK off pieces of dough the size of walnuts
and roll them into balls, oiling your hands lightly to
prevent the dough sticking. Press the balls in the
extra sesame seeds and flatten slightly. Lift
carefully so that the topping is not disturbed and
place, sesame seeds side up, on the baking
trays, spacing them 5 cm (2 in) apart to allow for
spreading. Bake for 15–20 minutes, or until golden.
Leave on the trays for 10 minutes before removing
to a wire rack to cool. Store in an airtight container.

Toast the sesame seeds in a
heavy-based pan for even heat
distribution, stirring often, then
tip immediately into a bowl to
prevent seeds from burning.

THE FOOD OF MOROCCO

GHORIBA

SEMOLINA BISCUITS

GHORIBA ARE BAKED FROM THE MIDDLE EAST TO MOROCCO. INGREDIENTS VARY A LITTLE; THIS MOROCCAN VERSION USES VERY FINE SEMOLINA AS WELL AS FLOUR, BUT YOU CAN REPLACE IT WITH PLAIN FLOUR IF THE REQUIRED SEMOLINA IS UNAVAILABLE (SEE GLOSSARY).

250 g (9 oz) unsalted butter
150 g (5½ oz/1¼ cups) plain (all-purpose) flour
125 g (4½ oz/1 cup) icing (confectioners') sugar
250 g (9 oz/2 cups) very fine semolina
2 eggs, beaten
1 teaspoon natural vanilla extract
1 egg white, lightly beaten
30 g (1 oz/¼ cup) split, blanched almonds

MAKES ABOUT 48

MELT the butter in a heavy-based saucepan over low heat. Skim off the froth, then pour into a mixing bowl, leaving the white milk solids in the pan. Set aside until cool.

SIFT the flour and icing sugar into a bowl, add the semolina and a pinch of salt and mix thoroughly. When the butter is cool but still liquid, stir in the eggs and vanilla, then add the dry ingredients, mixing to a firm dough. Knead well, then cover the bowl with plastic wrap and leave for 1 hour. Line two baking trays with baking paper. Preheat the oven to 180°C (350°F/Gas 4).

KNEAD the dough again until smooth and pliant. Take 3 level teaspoons of dough and shape into a smooth ball, then shape the remaining dough into balls of the same size. Place on prepared trays 2½ cm (1 in) apart, as these do not spread. Brush the tops lightly with egg white and press an almond on top of each biscuit, which will also help to flatten the biscuits a little. Bake for 20 minutes, or until lightly golden in colour. Cool on trays. When cold, store in an airtight container.

To clarify butter, melt in a pan – when frothing subsides, milk solids sink to the bottom. Skim and pour the clear oil into a bowl, leaving milk solids in the pan.

This 'assembly line' method of filling and shaping pastries works well, especially if making large quantities.

KAAB EL GHZAL
GAZELLES' HORNS

THESE ARE THE MOST POPULAR PASTRIES IN MOROCCO, SOLD AT STREET STALLS AND IN PATISSERIES, AND, ON FESTIVE OCCASIONS, MADE IN ENORMOUS QUANTITIES BY GROUPS OF WOMEN. THE PASTRY SHRINKS AROUND THE FILLING DURING BAKING, ALLOWING THE FILLING TO DOMINATE.

PASTRY
300 g (10½ oz/2½ cups) plain
   (all-purpose) flour
1 egg yolk
30 g (1 oz) butter, melted
2 tablespoons orange flower water

ALMOND FILLING
300 g (10½ oz/3 cups) ground
   almonds
90 g (3¼ oz/¾ cup) icing
   (confectioners') sugar, plus extra
   to dust
1 tablespoon orange flower water
1 egg white, lightly beaten
30 g (1 oz) unsalted butter, melted
½ teaspoon ground cinnamon
¼ teaspoon almond extract

MAKES ABOUT 28

TO MAKE pastry, sift flour into a mixing bowl and make a well in the centre. Beat the egg yolk into 125 ml (4 fl oz/½ cup) water and pour into flour with the butter and the orange flower water. Mix to a soft dough, then knead in bowl for 5 minutes to form a smooth, elastic dough. Divide in half, wrap in plastic wrap and rest for 20 minutes.

TO MAKE the almond filling, mix filling ingredients to a stiff paste. Take 3 level teaspoons of filling, shape into a ball, then shape remaining almond paste into balls of the same size. Roll each ball between your palms into logs 7½ cm (3 in), tapering at each end. Place on baking paper and set aside. Preheat oven to 180°C (350°F/Gas 4).

ROLL out one ball of dough thinly on a lightly floured work surface, to a rectangle about 30 x 40 cm (12 x 16 in), with the shorter side towards you. Place three almond shapes 5 cm (2 in) from edge of pastry closest to you and 2½ cm (1 in) apart and half that from each end. Lightly brush pastry along edge and between almond shapes with cold water. Lift and stretch end of pastry over the filling and press firmly around filling to seal. Cut around filling with fluted pastry wheel, leaving a 1 cm (½ in) border of pastry around filling. As each pastry is placed on the baking tray, bend it upwards on filling side into a crescent. Prick tops in four places with a cocktail pick. Straighten edge of pastry with a knife and repeat until all filling and pastry is used, including trimmings.

BAKE in oven for 12–15 minutes until cooked but still pale. Transfer to a wire rack and dust with sifted icing sugar while hot. Store in an airtight container when cool.

MINT FRESHNESS The most enticing aromas and sights of any Moroccan souk are the mint-laden carts (above left) or stalls. Spearmint (*Mentha spicata* or *M. viridis*), or Moroccan mint (*M. crispa*) are the only mints suitable for this national infusion. When in season, lemon verbena with blossoms (above right) is sold at fresh herb stalls; a sprig or two added to the teapot gives a lemony tang.

TEA CEREMONY

MOST OF THE HERBS IN MOROCCO ARE NATIVE TO THE MEDITERRANEAN REGION AND THE MIDDLE EAST. HERBAL INFUSIONS HAVE ALWAYS BEEN POPULAR IN MOROCCO. MINT GROWS THERE PARTICULARLY WELL, WITH MINT TEA TAKEN FOR INDIGESTION AND AS A CALMATIVE.

During the Crimean War in 1854, embargoes prevented British tea merchants selling to their usual customers and they looked elsewhere for new markets. Two of these were Tangier and Mogador. The Moroccans embraced tea drinking with enthusiasm, and soon found that the pale greenish brew perfectly complemented their favoured mint infusion. The preferred tea is Chinese gunpowder green tea. The teapot (*barrad*) is similar to that of the British 'Manchester' in shape, with a bulbous body, a domed lid and a long spout which is ideal for pouring the tea from a height with accuracy. It is made in silver plate, aluminium or stainless steel.

Besides mint, ingredients such as lemon verbena (see above), saffron, orange blossoms or cinnamon and wormwood are used in certain areas for additional flavour. However, it is the type of mint that is important. In Morocco they use a variety of spearmint that is known as Moroccan mint, *Mentha crispa*. Its leaves are not as slender as spearmint, *M. spicata*, and are more crinkled and a deeper green in colour. However spearmint is just as acceptable. Just as important is the tea; Chinese gunpowder green tea is the preferred tea. Each tea leaf is rolled into a compact, round

MAKING MINT TEA High-quality sugar is required, usually purchased as a tall cone about 20 cm (8 in) high and wrapped in purple tissue; lumps are broken from the cone with a special hammer. However, lump sugar in small oblongs is also used. Chinese gunpowder green tea is the preferred tea. The teapot is warmed with boiling water, the tea added and a little boiling water poured in, swirled and the

Mint tea is served in cafés (above left and centre), poured from a height to create a froth; other purveyors of the brew (above right) also provide mint tea to shop owners for their own refreshment, or to seal a deal with a customer. Young men carrying trays with glasses of mint tea, are a common sight in the souks, as nearby stallholders also take advantage of this service.

pellet. An alternative is Hyson; again individual small tea leaves are rolled up and twisted. When the tea is brewed, the tea leaves open up like tiny flower petals, so there is no need to strain it. The mint in the pot does a good job of that anyway.

The tea ceremony illustrated below is the home version, with the sugar cone shown to stress its importance in a more formal tea ceremony, carried out after entertaining dinner guests. Equipment is set out on a low, round table – a silver three-legged tray holding patterned tea glasses, a silver teapot, a brass hammer for breaking lumps from the sugar cone, and silver boxes for tea, mint and sugar lumps. With the boiling water from a *samovar*, the ritual is as described below. The tea is poured into each glass from a height to aerate it. Etiquette decrees that each guest has three glasses. And how do you drink tea from a glass? Grip its rim with the thumb and forefinger of the right hand and sip, sip, sip …

water carefully poured off to remove any tea dust. The pot is then half-filled with washed and dried fresh mint sprigs. Boiling water is poured in, the sugar lumps added and the lid replaced while it brews for three minutes. Tea is poured into a glass then returned to the pot three times, to mix the brew and check the colour. It is served very hot.

ATAY BIL NA'NA'

MINT TEA

THE NATIONAL BEVERAGE OF MOROCCO IS OMNIPRESENT – SERVED IN THE HOME, AT CAFES, IN RESTAURANTS, AND BREWED BY FIELD WORKERS. WHEN SELECTING A CARPET OR HAGGLING OVER A LEATHER JACKET, A PROFFERED GLASS OF MINT TEA IS PART OF THE BARGAINING PROCESS.

1 bunch fresh spearmint
2 teaspoons Chinese gunpowder green tea
2 tablespoons white sugar, or to taste

SERVES 4–6

CUT the ends of the mint stalks leaving leafy sprigs. Wash well, shake dry and roll in a tea towel (dish towel) to absorb excess moisture. Alternatively, dry mint in a salad spinner.

RINSE a 1 litre (36 fl oz/4 cup) teapot with boiling water, add the tea and a little boiling water, swirl briefly, let it settle, then carefully pour out the water to remove any tea dust. Half-fill pot with boiling water. Take a handful of the spearmint sprigs, crush lightly in the hand and add to the pot. Add more crushed mint sprigs until the pot is three-quarters full. Add the sugar and fill the pot with boiling water. Let the tea brew for 3 minutes.

POUR out a glass of tea and pour back into the pot. Repeat, twice more to mix the tea and to dissolve the sugar. Serve the tea in tea glasses, pouring it from a height to aerate the tea. Add an uncrushed mint sprig to each glass.

HLEEB B'LOOZ

ALMOND MILK DRINK

THERE ARE TWO VERSIONS OF ALMOND DRINK – ONE CONTAINING MILK AND THE OTHER USING WATER ONLY (SHARBAT B'LOOZ). THE MILK VERSION IS THE MOST DELICIOUS. TRADITIONALLY, THE ALMONDS ARE PULVERISED WITH SUGAR IN A MORTAR, BUT A BLENDER MAKES THE PROCESS EASIER.

235 g (8½ oz/1½ cups) fresh
  blanched almonds
55 g (2 oz/¼ cup) caster (superfine)
  sugar, or to taste
¼ teaspoon almond extract
½ teaspoon rosewater
250 ml (9 fl oz/1 cup) cold milk

SERVES 4

PUT the almonds and sugar in a blender with 250 ml (9 fl oz/1 cup) water. Blend until the almonds are well pulverised.

LINE a strainer with a double layer of muslin (cheesecloth), place over a bowl and pour the almond mixture into the strainer. Add 3 tablespoons water to the blender and blend briefly to clean the blender of any almond residue. Pour into the strainer. Press the almonds to extract as much moisture as possible, gather up the muslin, twist the end and squeeze firmly over the bowl, taking care that the almonds are safely enclosed. Place the muslin and almonds in the strainer again, add another 3 tablespoons water, stir and squeeze the almonds again. Discard the almonds.

STIR in the almond extract, rosewater and milk, taste and add a little more sugar if necessary. Chill and serve. (If you can find them, float an unsprayed fragrant pink rose petal or two on top of each drink.)

Hand-power is required to extract the almond milk from its muslin 'bag'. Wash hands well before making this delicious, fragrant drink.

'ASSEER DEL ZHIB WA MA'EL WARD
GRAPE JUICE WITH ROSEWATER

BLACK GRAPES GIVE A PLEASING COLOUR TO THIS DELICIOUS DRINK. FORTUNATELY MANY SEEDLESS GRAPE VARIETIES ARE AVAILABLE. GREEN GRAPES MAY ALSO BE USED FOR A PLEASANT BUT LIGHTER FLAVOURED BEVERAGE – OMIT THE CINNAMON.

500 g (1 lb 2 oz) chilled seedless
  black grapes
1 teaspoon rosewater
ground cinnamon, to serve (optional)

SERVES 2

WASH grapes very well and pull from stems. Drain well and feed grapes into juice extractor, catching the juice in a pitcher. When the grapes are juiced, let the grape juice settle and skim off any dark froth. Cover the pitcher with plastic wrap and chill in refrigerator for at least 1 hour.

DECANT juice into two tall glasses leaving any sediment in pitcher. Stir ½ teaspoon rosewater into each glass and dust top lightly with cinnamon, if desired.

'ASSEER DALAAH BIL MA'EL WARD
WATERMELON JUICE WITH ROSEWATER

WATERMELON JUICE IS A GREAT SUMMERTIME FAVOURITE, AND NOT ONLY IN MOROCCO. HOWEVER, THE ADDITION OF ROSEWATER TO THE JUICE TURNS A PLEASANT DRINK INTO A DIVINE ONE ON A HOT DAY. WIPE THE SKIN WITH A DAMP CLOTH BEFORE REMOVING THE SUCCULENT RED FLESH.

WATERMELON JUICE WITH ROSEWATER

1.5 kg (3 lb 5 oz) watermelon
1 teaspoon rosewater

SERVES 2–3

CHILL the watermelon thoroughly. Remove the rind and cut the pink part only into thick chunks that will fit into the juice extractor feed tube. Extract the juice into a pitcher. Take care when extracting the juice, as the seeds have a tendency to jump out of the feed tube.

ADD the rosewater and pour into two tall glasses, or store the juice in the refrigerator until ready to serve.

BASICS

Pour water onto regular couscous in bowl, stir, drain off and leave 15 minutes; stir occasionally. Between steamings, traditionally the couscous grains are rubbed with the hands to break up lumps. Fork through the couscous while steaming.

KSEKSOU

COUSCOUS (STEAMING METHOD)

BOTH REGULAR COUSCOUS AND INSTANT COUSCOUS SHOULD BE PREPARED IN THE SAME WAY – STEAMING THE GRAINS TO MAKE THEM LIGHT AND FLUFFY. THE TRADITIONAL METHOD OF RUBBING GRAINS TO REMOVE LUMPS AND 'AIR' THE GRAINS HAS BEEN REPLACED WITH A MODERN METHOD.

500 g (1 lb 2 oz/2¾ cups) regular
  couscous (see page 289)
90 g (3 oz) smen or herbed smen
  (page 282) or butter, diced

SERVES 6–8

PUT couscous in a large, shallow bowl, cover with cold water, stir with a balloon whisk and pour water off immediately through a strainer to catch any grains. Return grains to the bowl and set aside for 10 minutes to allow couscous to swell, stirring occasionally with the balloon whisk to keep grains separate.

USE the steamer section of a *couscoussier*, a steamer that fits snugly over a large saucepan, or a metal colander. If steamer does not fit snugly, put a long, folded strip of foil around the rim of the pan, place steamer in position and press firmly.

IF STEAMER has large holes, line with a double layer of muslin (cheesecloth). Spread couscous grains in steamer and place over the pan of food being cooked, or over a saucepan of boiling water. The base of the steamer must not touch the top of the stew or water. Cook until steam rises through the grains, cover and steam for 20 minutes. Fork through couscous occasionally to steam it evenly.

TIP the couscous into the bowl, add smen and ½ teaspoon salt and sprinkle with 125 ml (4 fl oz/ ½ cup) cold water. Stir again with the balloon whisk to separate grains. At this stage, couscous may be covered with a damp cloth and left several hours if necessary. About 20 minutes before stew is cooked, return couscous to steamer and replace over stew or boiling water. Do not cover while steaming and fluff up occasionally with a fork. Turn into the bowl, stir well with the balloon whisk and serve according to recipe.

INSTANT COUSCOUS: Follow above directions but only steam for 10 minutes each time.

ROZZ ZA'FRAN

SAFFRON RICE

ANDALUSIAN INFLUENCE IS OBVIOUS IN THIS RICE DISH, WHICH IS POPULAR IN NORTHERN MOROCCO. WHILE MOROCCANS STEAM THE RICE – A LENGTHY PROCESS – THE FOLLOWING USES THE ABSORPTION METHOD. A SHORT OR MEDIUM GRAIN IS THE TYPE USED IN MOROCCO.

500 g (1 lb 2 oz/2½ cups) short-grain rice
2 tablespoons olive oil
¼ teaspoon ground saffron threads
20 g (¾ oz) butter

SERVES 6

WASH the rice in a sieve until water runs clear, then drain well.

OVER medium heat, heat the oil in a heavy-based saucepan and add the rice, stirring so that all the rice is coated evenly with oil. Add 900 ml (31 fl oz/3⅔ cups) water, the saffron and ¼ teaspoon salt and stir well. Bring to the boil over high heat and boil for 1 minute.

REDUCE heat to low, cover and cook for 10–12 minutes or until all the water has been absorbed. Steam tunnels will form holes on the surface of the rice. Turn off heat, then leave the pan, covered, for 10 minutes. Add the butter and fluff lightly with a fork. Transfer to serving bowl. Saffron rice is used to accompany fish dishes, but can be used as a substitute for couscous.

Stir rice into heated oil and stir over heat until it becomes opaque, then add the liquid.

MARQA DEL HOUT

FISH STOCK

AFTER FILLETING WHOLE FISH, HEAD AND BONE REMAINS ARE PERFECT FOR MAKING STOCK. CHOOSE DEEP-SEA FISH – ESTUARY BOTTOM-FEEDERS HAVE A MUDDY TASTE. STORE IN FREEZER FOR 'INSTANT' USE. IF BOTTLED CLAM JUICE IS AVAILABLE IN YOUR REGION, USE THIS IN PLACE OF THE STOCK.

1 kg (2 lb 4 oz) fish heads and bones
1 small white onion, sliced
1 carrot, sliced
4 parsley stalks
1 small leafy celery stalk, roughly chopped
6 black peppercorns

MAKES 1.25 litres (44 fl oz/5 cups)

REMOVE gills and any blood from fish heads and rinse well in cold water with the bones. Place in a stock pot and add onion, carrot, parsley and celery. Cover with 1.5 litres (52 fl oz/6 cups) water. Over medium heat, bring slowly to simmering point, skimming as required. Add peppercorns and 1 teaspoon salt and simmer for 20 minutes. Strain though a sieve lined with muslin (cheesecloth) into a bowl, cover and refrigerate until required. Keeps up to 4 days in refrigerator, or freeze for up to 2 months.

FISH STOCK

CLARIFIED BUTTER

BUTTER IS MELTED AND HEATED FOR A LENGTHY TIME UNTIL THE MILK SOLIDS SINK AND BEGIN TO BROWN, GIVING A NUTTY FLAVOUR. FOR TRADITIONAL CLARIFIED BUTTER, SKIM THE FROTH AND POUR THE CLEAR FAT INTO A CONTAINER BEFORE THE MILK SOLIDS BROWN. GHEE IS A SUBSTITUTE.

250 g (9 oz) salted or unsalted
  butter, diced

MAKES 175 G (6 OZ)

PUT the butter in a heavy-based saucepan over low heat. If using gas, place over the smallest burner with a heat diffuser, as butter has a tendency to spit if the heat is not low enough.

SIMMER very gently for 25 minutes. Pour through a sieve lined with muslin (cheesecloth), set over a bowl. The clear oil is the smen and has a slightly nutty taste. Store in a sealed jar in the refrigerator, although it can safely be stored at room temperature, as is done in Morocco. This keeps for many months.

FOR sweet pastries using filo, smen is recommended, even with its slightly nutty flavour, because if melted unclarified butter is used any milk solids brushed onto the filo become dark when cooked, spoiling the appearance of the baked pastry.

As the butter bubbles, the froth sinks. When the milk solids begin to colour, strain into a bowl.

HERBED CLARIFIED BUTTER

TRADITIONALLY, THIS IS STORED IN A STONE JAR AND BURIED FOR A YEAR OR MORE, GIVING IT A STRONG CHEESY FLAVOUR. IT IS MUCH LOVED STIRRED THROUGH COUSCOUS. A SHORT CUT IS TO MIX TOGETHER EQUAL QUANTITIES OF HERBED SMEN AND BLUE CHEESE.

2 tablespoons dried za'atar, or dried
  Greek thyme
2 teaspoons coarse salt
250 g (9 oz) salted or unsalted
  butter

MAKES 175 G (6 OZ)

PUT the za'atar and salt in a sieve lined with muslin (cheesecloth). Following the directions above, heat the butter and slowly pour it through the herb and salt mixture. Store in a sealed jar in the refrigerator. In Morocco, herbed smen is aged for months, even years, and has a strong, cheesy flavour. This is a milder version.

HERBED SMEN

HAMED MARKAD
PRESERVED LEMONS

MAKE PRESERVED LEMONS WITH RIPE, NEW-SEASON FRUIT THAT HAVE NOT BEEN WAXED. STORE-BOUGHT LEMONS ARE USUALLY COATED WITH A WAX, WHICH HAS TO BE REMOVED BY SCRUBBING IN WARM WATER WITH A SOFT-BRISTLE BRUSH; EVEN THEN IT IS VERY DIFFICULT TO REMOVE.

8–12 thin-skinned new-season
   lemons
rock salt
1–2 extra lemons
black peppercorns, optional
bay leaves, optional

FILLS 1 X 2 LITRE (70 FL OZ/
8 CUPS) JAR OR 2 X 1 LITRE
35 FL OZ/4 CUPS) JARS

TO PREPARE a storage jar, preheat the oven to 120°C (235°F/Gas ½). Wash the jar and lid in hot soapy water and rinse with hot water. Put the jar in the oven for 20 minutes, or until fully dry. Do not dry with a tea towel (dish towel).

IF LEMONS are very firm, soak in water to cover for 3 days, changing water daily. Wash lemons if soaking is not required. Cut lemons from the stem end into quarters almost to the base. Insert 1 tablespoon rock salt into each lemon, close it up and place in a jar. Repeat until jar is filled, sprinkling 1 tablespoon salt between layers. Pack lemons into the jar as tightly as possible and add a bay leaf and a few black peppercorns to each jar if desired.

WASH extra lemons and add the juice of 1 lemon to each jar. Fill with slightly cooled, boiled water. Put the washed skin from a squeezed-out lemon half on top so that if any white film forms on top (which is harmless), the lemon skin can be discarded when the jar is opened. Seal and store in a cool, dark place for 4 weeks, gently shaking jars daily for the first week to dissolve the salt. The cloudy liquid clears in this time. Lemons will keep for 6 months or more. Once jar is opened, store in the refrigerator.

TO PREPARE FOR COOKING: Remove a lemon with a clean fork. Separate lemon into quarters and rinse under running water. Remove the pulp and discard. Rinse the rind, pat dry with paper towel and use as directed in recipes.

To prepare for recipes, rinse preserved lemon, remove pulp with a spoon. Rinse rind and pat dry with paper towel, then cut as directed.

HARISSA

HOT CHILLI PASTE

HARISSA IS EXTREMELY HOT, SO YOU SHOULD USE WITH CAUTION. FOR A MILDER VERSION OF THIS FIERY PASTE, SLIT THE CHILLIES (INSTEAD OF CHOPPING THEM) BEFORE SOAKING IN THE BOILING WATER. THEN SCRAPE OUT THE SEEDS BEFORE PROCESSING AS PER THE RECIPE.

125 g (4½ oz) dried red chillies,
   stems removed
1 tablespoon dried mint
1 tablespoon ground coriander
1 tablespoon ground cumin
1 teaspoon ground caraway seeds
10 garlic cloves, chopped
125 ml (4 fl oz/½ cup) olive oil

FILLS A 600 ML
(21 FL OZ/2½ CUPS) JAR

TO PREPARE a storage jar, preheat the oven to 120°C (235°F/Gas ½). Wash the jar and lid in hot soapy water and rinse with hot water. Put the jar in the oven for 20 minutes, or until fully dry. Do not dry with a tea towel (dish towel).

ROUGHLY chop the chillies, then cover with boiling water and soak for 1 hour. Drain, put them in a food processor and add the mint, spices, garlic, 1 tablespoon of the olive oil and ½ teaspoon salt. Process for 20 seconds, scrape down the side of the bowl, then process for another 30 seconds. With the motor running, gradually add the remaining oil. Scrape down the side of the bowl when necessary.

SPOON the paste into the clean jar, cover with a thin layer of olive oil and seal. Label and date. Harissa will keep in the refrigerator for up to 6 months.

Chop the dried chillies before soaking. The food processor makes short work of preparing harissa.

RAS EL HANOUT

SPICE BLEND

½ teaspoon ground cloves
½ teaspoon ground cayenne
   pepper
2 teaspoons ground allspice
2 teaspoons ground cumin
2 teaspoons ground ginger
2 teaspoons ground turmeric
2 teaspoons ground black pepper
2 teaspoons ground cardamom
3 teaspoons ground cinnamon
3 teaspoons ground coriander
2 nutmegs, freshly grated (or
   6 teaspoons ground nutmeg)

PURCHASE the freshest spices possible of a reliable brand, or purchase from a specialist spice store. Combine all the ground spices in a clean jar, seal and store in a cool, dark place. Alternatively, use whole spices in the same quantities and grind in a spice grinder. However, grate the nutmegs separately as most grinders cannot cope with them. Makes 60 g (2¼ oz).

RAS EL HANOUT

GLOSSARY OF MOROCCAN FOOD AND COOKING

almonds Whole, slivered and ground almonds are often used in sweet and savoury dishes. If ground almonds (almond meal) are not available, use whole or slivered almonds and grind in a food processor. Use very fresh, dry almonds for this, and process them as briefly as possible to prevent them from becoming oily; for this reason, slivered almonds are the better option. Pack well when using cup measures, as freshly ground almonds are lighter in texture than the packaged variety.

almonds, blanched Almonds keep better if purchased with skin on and have a better flavour when freshly blanched. To blanch, place in a bowl, cover with boiling water and leave for 5 minutes, drain and slip off skins when cool. Spread onto a paper towel–lined baking tray and leave until dry and crisp, or put in a slow oven for 5 minutes to dry thoroughly. Store in a sealed container in the refrigerator.

almonds, green These appear in souks in mid-summer, when the drupe is green and the almond shell is still soft within – test with a pin. They are left to soak in salted water for a day or two, then eaten whole as a snack.

aniseed Also known as anise seed, the pale brown seeds have a mild liquorice flavour. It is a popular flavouring and topping for bread. It is also used in sweet, rusk-like toasts called *fekkas* –

sweet yeast bread baked, then sliced next day and crisped in the oven. Most households have *fekkas* on hand to have with their morning mint tea.

broad (fava) beans Only very young fresh, shelled beans are used in tagines; if more mature, peel the beans and reduce cooking time. Dried broad beans are often used to make a bean soup or dip; they need to be first soaked for 48 hours in a cool place such as the refrigerator, changing water 3–4 times, and the leathery skins removed before use. Dried, skinned broad beans are sold in North African and Middle Eastern food markets as skinned *ful* beans and will save time in preparation.

capsicum This is also given as 'pepper' in recipes. In Morocco they use a sweet pepper that is thinner-fleshed, not as broad as a capsicum, and tapering to a point. The *Capsicum* genus also includes chillies.

chard Also known as silverbeet and Swiss chard, it is a member of the beet family. The leaves are bright green and crinkly in texture, with a white rib running through the leaf widening into a stem. It is much loved by North African and Middle Eastern people, probably as it grows prolifically in their gardens.

chickpeas Skinned chickpeas are preferred as they absorb flavours better. Soak chickpeas overnight; the next day,

lift up handfuls of chickpeas and rub them between your hands to loosen the skins, then skim the skins off as they float. Cover the chickpeas with fresh water and boil for at least an hour, until tender, or add to a stew or soup at the start of cooking. Tinned chickpeas may also be used, with skins removed in the same way. If preferred, leave skins on for all recipes as modern Moroccan cooks do. However, if you find that pulses disagree with you, try the skinned chickpeas. In terms of measurements, 220 g (7¾ oz/1 cup) dried chickpeas yields 2½ cups cooked, which is equivalent to 2 x 420 g (15 oz) tins.

cinnamon Finely shaved bark from the cinnamon tree, *Cinnamomum zeylanicum*, which is interleaved and rolled to form sticks or quills. Both sticks and ground cinnamon are widely used. Ground cinnamon often includes cassia, which is actually from another species of cinnamon tree. Cassia is more reddish-brown than cinnamon and can be used in place of cinnamon sticks; in fact, it is often sold as such. Cinnamon is used in savoury and sweet dishes and pastries.

coriander (cilantro) Essential in Moroccan cooking, fresh coriander has feathery green leaves with a somewhat pungent flavour. Coriander seeds are ground and used as a spice.

corn on the cob A popular street food, the sweet corn is cut from the plant leaving a portion of the stem attached. Cobs are husked with the silk removed and grilled over a charcoal fire. Before it is handed to the customer, the hot grilled cob is dipped in salted water which makes it moist and very tasty, with a convenient handle already attached.

cornmeal, yellow Dried yellow corn kernels ground to a meal, available in fine, medium and coarse grades from health food stores; choose the medium grade. Do not confuse with polenta, which is a granular form and not used in Morocco. Cornmeal is used to add to bread in rural areas, or for sprinkling on baking trays or on top of loaves to add crunch and flavour.

couscous Made with coarse semolina grains and durum wheat flour. Semolina grains are sprinkled with lightly salted water and rolled with flour to form tiny pellets. This is still done by hand by some cooks, but these days machines are used. Both couscous purchased in bulk (regular couscous) and packets of instant couscous require steaming for the grains to swell properly and become light and fluffy. Regular couscous is found in Middle Eastern food stores; in supermarkets couscous is usually instant; if packet is marked 'Maghrebi-style', it is regular couscous.

couscoussier The French name for the utensil in which couscous is steamed; in Moroccan the base is *qadra* and the top steamer is *keskes*, but the French name is in popular use even in Morocco. The base is tall and slightly bulbous, with the steamer section fitted on top for cooking couscous. The traditional *couscoussier* of tin-lined copper does not have a lid, but the aluminium version usually does. The original *couscoussier* of the Berbers was earthenware.

cumin With a warm, sweet aroma, yet pungent and earthy, cumin is one of the most popular spices in the region. Always select a darker cumin with a greenish-brown colour and oily texture. For the best flavour, use freshly ground seeds. A mixture of cumin and salt is a favourite condiment; for street food, it accompanies boiled eggs, pieces of *mechoui* (spit-roasted lamb), lamb kebabs and lamb liver kebabs. At the table, little bowls of the mixture are provided, especially if steamed chicken or lamb is served.

figs This remarkable fruit has been important to the Mediterranean region from early days. The fresh fruit, both the purple (black) variety and the green, begins to appear early in summer. The majority of figs, however, are consumed dried and are found in souk stalls strung on dried date-palm fronds like necklaces. The fresh fruit is enjoyed as an ending to a meal, the dried for snacking, cooking and combined with dates for sweet pastry fillings.

filo pastry This thin pastry of the Eastern Mediterranean is not Moroccan, but it is the most easily available substitute outside Morocco for *warkha* pastry. Certain measurements have been given in recipes regarding sheet and strip sizes, and these will serve as a guide for the size available in your area. However, most important of all is how it is handled. Thaw as directed on package if frozen; whether frozen or chilled, it must be left in its package at room temperature for 2 hours before opening and unfolding the sheets. Place the sheets flat on your work surface, and while working with them, keep the sheets covered with dry, folded cloths or plastic sheeting; never put damp cloths in contact with the pastry. Keep the kitchen cool and draught-free if possible.

gharbal A sieve which is today made from metal mesh, but which used to be made of pierced leather. It is used for sifting couscous grains as they are made; the larger particles are returned to the *gsaa* for reworking. Also used for other sifting purposes.

ginger Only dried ginger is used in Moroccan cooking, never fresh. Do not use more than is given in recipes as too much ginger can impart a bitter taste.

gsaa A large, shallow wooden or earthenware bowl in which bread is kneaded or couscous grains made. An earthenware *gsaa* is also used for soaking couscous before cooking, and for rubbing and separating the grains during and after cooking.

gum arabic Little tears of dried sap from *Acacia arabica* and other trees of the family *Mimosoideae*. It is sometimes wrongly given in recipes, when mastic is the spice that should be used. However, gum arabic is used to flavour water; a few tears are thrown on the embers of a brazier, and an unglazed pitcher is inverted over the fumes and left for a time so that the aroma penetrates the pitcher. Water is stored in the pitcher and absorbs the aroma.

harissa A Tunisian condiment popular in Morocco, harissa is available from gourmet food stores and Middle Eastern markets, or make your own (page 286). Use with caution as it is extremely hot.

honey Good Moroccan honeys are thick and aromatic with the flavour of herbs. If you can't find Moroccan honey, use Mount Hymettus or other Greek thyme honey. Orange blossom honey is light and fragrant and is readily available.

mastic Tears of resin from a small evergreen tree that grows in regions of the Mediterranean, especial the Greek island of Chios. Used to flavour sweet pastries, especially in Marrakesh, where it is added to almond paste for filling pastries. Do not confuse with gum arabic – this is an incense and a glue.

merguez A lamb sausage of Tunisian origin, popular in Morocco. It is spiced with harissa, paprika, allspice, fennel, black pepper, cumin and coriander seeds and flavoured with garlic. It is usually very hot, but the degree of heat depends on the manufacturer.

nigella seeds These little black seeds are usually sprinkled on bread before baking, and on steamed chicken. They have little aroma, but have a nutty flavour and are a little peppery. Black cumin seeds and black sesame seeds are often mistakenly called nigella.

noodles See *sheriya*

olive oil Olive oil was, and is, used for salads, but there is an increasing trend in Morocco to replace smen in cooking with olive or other oils in the interests of better health. While specified throughout, as a general rule, extra virgin olive oil is recommended for salads, and the standard olive oil for cooking. Other vegetable oils are usually used for frying – sunflower, safflower and peanut (ground nut).

onion The brown onion is the one used in most Moroccan cooking. Occasionally white onion is used; red onion is used in salads. Green onion is used as an accompaniment to some soups such as *bissara* in certain areas.

orange flower water Also called orange blossom water, this is made from a distillation of the flowers of the bitter bigarade (seville) orange. It originated in the Middle East and was introduced to North Africa by the Arabs. Used to flavour beverages, and sweet and savoury food, it is also distilled in the home – see also 'rosewater'.

paprika The paprika commonly used is Spanish mild paprika. It is used as much for the colour as its flavour. Sweet Hungarian paprika may also be used.

parsley Flat-leaf (Italian) parsley is used. Alternatively, use curly parsley and include some stalks when chopping to increase its flavour in cooking.

pomegranate The Moroccans love colour, and the ruby red seeds of the pomegranate are used to scatter over fresh fruit platters. Pomegranate juice is a favourite drink, and a citrus juicer is the best way to extract it, especially the type that has a hinged press attached. Removing the seeds is tedious as they must be separated from the pith (usually a few hard taps on the outside of a cut pomegranate held over a bowl can accomplish this). Fruit-juice extractors can graze the seeds, giving the juice a bitter flavour. Serve the chilled juice with a little rosewater. The pomegranate syrup that is sold in Middle Eastern stores is not used in Morocco.

preserved lemons Used in tagines and many Moroccan dishes to give a distinctive flavour. Make your own (page 285) or buy those that are preserved in the Moroccan manner (no oil) from gourmet food stores or good delicatessens.

prunes The prune is the dried version of various species of the damascene (damson) plum. It is often a substitute for dates in meat and fruit tagines, but is increasingly used in its own right – an intensely flavoured sweet–sour fruit that marries well with spices. Today's prunes do not need soaking – they are moist and succulent and add a wonderful flavour to Moroccan dishes. While it is an easy (though somewhat sticky) task to remove the pits, pitted prunes are readily available.

quince A popular winter fruit used in tagines. While quince paste is not made in Morocco, it works very well in recipes when quinces are not in season.

ras el hanout A blend of many spices, which vary according to the maker. Some blends are kept a closely guarded secret. You can make your own version (page 286) or buy a ready-made ground spice mix from gourmet food stores or herb and spice stores.

rashasha An ornate flask of coloured glass with a rounded body and a tall and slender neck, ornately decorated with silver metalwork. It is filled with orange flower water or rosewater, and after the Moroccan ritual handwashing before and after a banquet or formal meal, the hands are lightly sprinkled with the flower water.

rice Short- or medium-grained rice is preferred. It is used mainly in the north – Tangier, Tetuan and environs – where there is a stronger Spanish influence. However, Moroccans steam rice three times in a *couscoussier*, or in a colander lined with muslin over boiling water. Traditional rice-cooking methods have been used in the recipes.

rosewater A distillation of fragrant rose petals, originating in Persia and introduced to North Africa by the Arabs. In May, fresh rose petals and rosebuds are sold in souks. Many locals distil their own using an *alembic*, a superseded distiller that remains in use in Morocco and the Middle East. Where obtainable, orange blossoms (see 'orange flower water') are also distilled. It is bottled and kept for 4–5 months before use and claimed to be superior to that made by distilleries. Rosewater is used to flavour beverages and sweet and savoury foods.

saffron The dried stigmas of *Crocus sativus*, regarded as the world's most expensive spice. Each flower consists of only three stigmas, which are hand-picked from the flowers, then dried. Introduced by the Arabs, it is grown, harvested and processed in Morocco. Threads and ground saffron are used as much for the beautiful yellow colour as for the aroma and flavour. Where a recipe calls for a pinch of ground saffron, use as much as sits on the very tip of a knife, as fingertips would take more than required. Only buy ground or powdered saffron from a reliable supplier.

290